LONGEVITY FOR CATS

ALSO BY GARY RICHTER, M.S., D.V.M., C.V.C., C.V.A.

The Ultimate Pet Health Guide: Breakthrough Nutrition and Integrative Care for Dogs and Cats

Longevity for Dogs: A Holistic, Individualized Approach to Helping Your Canine Companion Live Longer—and Healthier

Please visit:

Hay House USA: www.hayhouse.com®
Hay House Australia: www.hayhouse.com.au
Hay House UK: www.hayhouse.co.uk
Hay House India: www.hayhouse.co.in

Praise for

LONGEVITY FOR CATS

"As the guy who started the biohacking movement for humans, I'm so excited about Dr. Richter's book, Longevity for Cats. *Of course, we can also use biohacking to improve—and extend—the lives of our furry companions. In his book, Dr. Richter shares his vast knowledge and expertise on pet nutrition, exercise, and environmental enrichment. The strategies he outlines are not only effective, but they're also practical and easy to implement. So, if you're a pet owner who's interested in giving your furry friend the best possible life, then I highly recommend checking out* Longevity for Cats *by Dr. Richter. Your pets will thank you for it!"*

— **Dave Asprey**, father of biohacking, four-time *New York Times* best-selling author, host of *The Human Upgrade Podcast,* CEO of Upgrade Labs

"My cat may as well be my child; I love her with every ounce of my being! That's why I'm excited to now have a manual for how to keep her alive and healthy for as long as possible. Longevity for Cats *is a must-have book for anyone with a cat in the family. Don't wait, start meow!"*

— **Max Lugavere**, author of the *New York Times* best-seller *Genius Foods, The Genius Life*, and *Genius Kitchen*

"I have personally experienced how Dr. Gary Richter's approach to pet care has enhanced the longevity and vitality of my fur babies, and I am forever grateful! His new book, Longevity for Cats, *empowers pet parents through science-backed nutrition, supplementation, exercise, and lifestyle recommendations to help their four-legged family members live long and happy lives. I highly recommend this book as a resource and look forward to a fast-approaching world where humans and pets are aging well, together."*

— **Serena Poon, C.N., C.H.C., C.H.N.**, CEO and founder of Serena Loves LLC and Just Add Water; co-founder of Fully Aligned Co LLC

"Gary Richter is a gift to the veterinary world. He understands not only pet health but has now elegantly translated insights from human longevity medicine into the pet world with clarity and practicality. If you want more great years with your cat, you'll love this book!"

— **Jeffrey Gladden, M.D. F.A.C.C.**, founder and CEO of Gladden Longevity

"If you love your cat then you need this book. Death comes too soon to our four-legged friends, but now it doesn't have to. Dr. Richter has written a groundbreaking book providing a step-by-step guide to giving your loving companion not only more years but also a higher quality of life. Dr. Richter is a thoughtful, kind, and brilliant medical professional who is a veterinary's vet that everybody wishes they had as their own personal physician. His book Longevity for Cats *provides not only a clear explanation of the science of longevity but is also a practical guide to the steps you can take now to ensure your pets will have the longest, healthiest life possible. Buy this book for your best friend. Buy this book for yourself, because keeping your best friend healthy helps keep you healthy."*

— **Dr. Gary Kaplan**, medical director, Kaplan Center for Integrative Medicine, Mclean, Virginia, clinical associate professor, Georgetown University School of Medicine, author of *Why You Are Still Sick: How Infections Can Break Your Immune System and How You Can Recover*

"Dr. Richter is one the leading experts on pet health, biohacking, and nutrition. This book is a groundbreaking resource that's taking tough (and brilliant) concepts and making them super simple."

— **Shawn Wells, M.P.H., R.D., L.D.N., C.I.S.S.N.**, biochemist, formulator, and international best-selling author of *The ENERGY Formula*

"We are on the threshold of a whole new age of how medical science views and upholds proper healthcare and longevity. This book nails it on the head. While being extremely comprehensive, Dr. Richter has kept a potentially boring and confusing subject easy to understand, while being a fascinating and enjoyable read. He welcomes us to the necessary future of medicine and healthcare for our companion animals and even us too."

— **Marty Goldstein, D.V.M.**, author of *The Nature of Animal Healing* and *The Spirit of Animal Healing*

"He's done it again—twice this time. My good friend and holistic veterinary colleague, Dr. Gary Richter, wrote his book The Ultimate Pet Health Guide: Breakthrough Nutrition and Integrative Care for Dogs and Cats *published by Hay House in 2017. Now he has two new books from Hay House,* Longevity for Cats *and* Longevity for Dogs. *They are both factually impressive, thorough, practical, and entertaining—does this man ever sleep?! I'm honored to be mentioned briefly within each of them."*

— **W. Jean Dodds, D.V.M.**

LONGEVITY FOR CATS

A HOLISTIC, INDIVIDUALIZED APPROACH TO HELPING YOUR FELINE FRIEND LIVE LONGER—AND HEALTHIER

GARY RICHTER, M.S., D.V.M.

HAY HOUSE INDIA
New Delhi • London • Sydney
Carlsbad, California • New York City

Published in India by: Hay House Publishers India: www.hayhouse.co.in
Published in the United States by: Hay House, Inc.: www.hayhouse.com®
Published in Australia by: Hay House Australia Pty. Ltd.: www.hay house.com.au
Published in the United Kingdom by: Hay House UK, Ltd.: www.hayhouse.co.uk

Project editor: Nicolette Salamanca Young • *Indexer:* Shapiro Indexing Services
Cover design: Valerie Ramsey • *Interior design:* Nick C. Welch

First Hay House India Edition 2024

ISBN: 978-81-19554-93-5

Printed at Repro India Limited

This book is dedicated to every animal who has shown me how to be a better healer and how to love unconditionally.

CONTENTS

INTRODUCTION

Our cats should live forever—or at least as long as we do. This sentiment is shared by pretty much every cat parent who comes into my office. The reality, of course, is cat ownership (or guardianship, if you prefer) is filled with years of loving and unforgettable experiences that end with devastating loss.

The death of a beloved kitty is a life-altering event. For many, the loss of a feline family member can be more impactful than the loss of a human family member. After all, we don't receive unconditional love from the humans in our life, and for those of us who aren't perfect (*all* of us), having a companion who forgives and forgets is a gift beyond measure. In my 25 years of practicing veterinary medicine, I have held hands with, hugged, and counseled scores of cat owners, with discussions about smooth transitions, quality of life, and how allowing our family member to have a peaceful and painless landing is the last, best favor we can do for them.

It's all true. Euthanasia as a last treatment option is both incredibly difficult and a wonderful gift. Anyone who has ever seen a family member (human or animal) in pain at the end of life will understand that transitioning before things get really bad is a blessing. But what if there was a way to help our pets live longer and healthier lives and delay those sad, final days by a few—or even many—years? What if there was a way to postpone that day indefinitely?

Longevity science for humans is a rapidly growing field of study that has attracted some of the best and brightest scientific minds. My first real exposure to longevity as an achievable goal began in 2020 with two specific events. The first was a trip to Dallas, where I met Dr. Jeffrey Gladden, an interventional cardiologist by training who has now turned his sights on improving the longevity and performance of his patients. Sitting down with Dr. Gladden and discussing what we know about longevity and how we can affect the multiple pathways in the body that impact aging brought into focus that longevity is now much more than a general concept. I realized that through diagnostic testing, diet, and the use of supplements—and sometimes pharmaceuticals and medical treatments—we can slow and frequently even reverse the ticking clock in our bodies.

The second revelation occurred with an unexpected phone call. My good friend Richard Rossi is the creator of an event called the Congress of Future Medical Leaders, which brings together thousands of high-achieving high-school students who have professional aspirations in medicine. Top doctors, scientists, and even Nobel Prize winners regularly present at this meeting. I have been blessed with being a speaker and have had the opportunity to shine a light on both veterinary medicine and holistic/integrative medicine for these future medical professionals. Richard's skill at creating and hosting an event is the best I have ever seen. When he called in 2020 to tell me he was assembling a small group of people to have in-depth discussions about longevity science, well, let's just say he "had me at hello."

As I write this, there have since been four meetings of the group, called DaVinci 50, and it has been an eye-opening experience. The group, capped at 50 participants, allows for up-close and personal discussions with the speakers and the other brilliant minds in the room. Some of the world's greatest scientists in longevity research—including David Sinclair, George Church, Aubrey de Grey, Greg Fahy, and more—have presented. The research has been, to say the least, cutting-edge, and I'll cover a lot of it in this book.

By the end of 2020, I was turning my own sights toward longevity medicine for pets. I've been practicing integrative medicine for decades, utilizing both conventional allopathic medicine and acupuncture, herbs, chiropractic hyperbaric oxygen, ozone, and other more holistic methods. I took my first steps down the pathway of integrative medicine because I didn't like telling pet owners that we had exhausted all treatment options and their only choice was to discuss end-of-life planning. The truth is that there are many beneficial alternative therapies—those outside of medication and surgery—that can be advantageous to our pets. As I learned about and implemented more ways to help my patients, I found that cats were living longer and better lives than they "should" have, based on what is expected from allopathic medicine alone. During these years practicing integrative medicine, I focused primarily on maintaining quality of life. Increasing quantity of life was an added bonus, but it wasn't until meeting Dr. Gladden and attending DaVinci 50 that I began to look at longevity as an achievable primary goal. Medical science has progressed to the point where we now understand many of the metabolic pathways in the body that affect aging, and through new diagnostic tests, we can gather actionable information to slow the aging process.

My goal in writing this book is to provide you, as your cat's companion and caregiver, with an accessible and actionable guide you can use to help your cat live a longer—and healthier—life. By necessity, we are going to discuss some science, but no Ph.D. or medical degree will be required to successfully read and, hopefully, enjoy this book. We will explore both currently accessible options and the cutting-edge science that will become available for humans and pets in the near future.

We are at an inflection point in science and medicine where the end of life may no longer be inevitable or, at the very least, will be delayed significantly. That may seem like an outrageous claim, but I encourage you to read on! Science is right on the brink of solving aging, and while the vast majority of this research has been focused on people, you and I both know that the lives of our cats are at least as important as our own silly human lives.

I hope you find this book as informative and enjoyable to read as it has been for me to write. Most important, may the information you find within these pages help you to help your cat(s) live their longest, healthiest life!

PART I

UNDERSTANDING LONGEVITY SCIENCE

CHAPTER 1

WHAT DOES "LONGEVITY" REALLY MEAN?

The average cat's life expectancy is somewhere between 12 and 18 years. The oldest cat I have ever personally seen was a patient who passed away at 26, and the oldest recorded in the *Guinness Book of World Records* was 38 years old at the time of her death.[1] But what if 38 was not a one-in-many-millions outlier? What if these ages became normal and expected life spans for our best friends? What if there was no time limit on our cats' life span at all? This is where the modern science of longevity comes in.

When you think of *longevity*, perhaps you imagine living a long and healthy life. Maybe it means you're remembered after you're gone or your family (and genetics) survives for many generations into the future. These are both viable perspectives on longevity, but for the purposes of this book, we are interested in something that has long been sought after by scientists, mystics, and theologians, with no success. At its most basic level, longevity science is about finding solutions that extend life not only to a dramatically advanced age but also potentially indefinitely.

Modern longevity science is a pretty new field, and a lot of the current research has been done in the laboratory on cell cultures or lab animals, ranging from nematodes (worms) to fruit flies to rodents. Most of the diagnostic and treatment strategies we will discuss have been designed for use in humans, although to be clear, they are working with the same lab-animal data we are. From a veterinary-medicine perspective, longevity science is about as new as it comes. Barely anyone in the veterinary profession is even thinking about diagnostics and treatments specifically targeting longevity for cats, although I promise you that will change in the near future. For now, much of the research, diagnostic testing, and therapies we discuss for your cat are based on what we know from the lab-animal data and what is occurring within the field of longevity medicine for humans.

Clearly, we all want our cats to live more years, but it really has to be about more than just quantity. I can tell you that the 26-year-old kitty who was a patient in my care was not in the best of shape for the last several years of her life. She had poor mobility, had lost most of her eyesight and hearing, and was not cognitively all there. Any of us who has seen what aging can do to the body and mind—whether feline or human—knows that purely living to an advanced age is not always ideal and comes with its own issues. Instead, longevity is about maintaining a high *quality* of life for the entire life span—what is sometimes referred to as *health span*. In other words, while we can't stop the aging process altogether (yet), we can work to avoid the health declines that come with it. My goal (and hopefully yours as well) is for cats to live far longer than the 10- to 14-year average *and* to maintain their youth and vigor until the end—increasing both quantity and quality of life.

All too frequently, aging cats and their people come into my office, and when I ask how the cat is doing, the response is, "She's doing great, just slowing down a little now that she is getting older." Slowing down is an external sign that body systems are beginning to function inefficiently. This may be due to arthritis, back pain, organ disease, cognitive impairment, or any number of other medical diagnoses. But this slowing down is often the first visible sign of a cat's decline. The truth is, once these changes are noticeable, they have been present for quite some time.

When investigating longevity for cats, by necessity we need to take a hard look at what aging is and what it does. I realize that can be a little difficult, because it is always more comfortable to not seriously consider a furry companion's mortality. But as with any challenge we encounter, the solution here requires an understanding of what went wrong and why. This is how we are going to approach longevity for cats. My goal as a veterinarian, and yours as a pet owner, is to prevent as many of these things from happening and to slow or reverse those that have already occurred. Modern medicine can already do some of this with things like stem cells and platelet-rich plasma, but where the science is *going* will blow your mind.

The history of humanity's search for a means to ward off death is about as old as human history itself. Over 2,200 years ago, the Chinese emperor Qin Shi Huang charged his subjects with finding a potion to give him eternal life.[2] Qin Shi Huang was certainly not alone in his quest. From the story of the immortal Gilgamesh in 600 B.C. to Ponce de León searching for the fountain of youth in the early 1500s to the cutting edge of modern longevity science, people have not let go of the idea of being able to extend life or completely ward off the inevitability of death. Though magical elixirs and fountains have largely been left in the rearview mirror, the question of longevity hasn't changed. People are still asking how to prolong youth, health, and life. But now, we can start by investigating the root of the problem: What are the processes that lead to physical and mental decline, aging, and ultimately death? In this chapter, I will introduce and explain the 14 hallmarks of aging so that you can begin to focus on how to prevent these processes from occurring in your beloved cat.

THE HALLMARKS OF AGING

Let's begin with an understanding of how aging works. At its core, aging is a loss of function that occurs over time and eventually leads to a body being incapable of maintaining life. This loss of function is due to a complicated web of entangled bodily processes, and the bad news is that there is not, and likely will never be, one magic pill to keep us—and our cats—young forever. Slowing or halting aging is a multifactorial process that requires addressing many different aspects of health on a cellular level.

One of the most comprehensive descriptions of the mechanics of aging can be found in a 2013 article in the medical journal *Cell*. Titled "The Hallmarks of Aging," it outlines nine specific categories that lead to loss of function, and most of the current research into life extension is directed at affecting one or more of these.[3] The categories sound pretty complicated (scientists tend to favor the complicated), but we'll break down what is crucial to understand. In large part, all the testing and treatment strategies discussed in the upcoming chapters will be focused on addressing one or more of these hallmarks: *genomic instability, telomere attrition, epigenetic alterations, loss of proteostasis, deregulated nutrient sensing, mitochondrial dysfunction, cellular senescence, stem cell exhaustion*, and *altered intercellular communication*.

More recently, at a symposium in Copenhagen in 2022, five more hallmarks of aging were introduced, bringing the total to 14: *compromised autophagy, microbiome disturbance, altered mechanical properties, splicing dysregulation*, and *inflammation.*[4] Some of the new categories, such as inflammation, were already described in the original nine but have now been made their own separate category. For the purposes of our longevity discussions, we will focus largely on the original nine hallmarks of aging, as they are the most well studied and provide good options for intervention.

Genomic Instability

The material responsible for all life on Earth is deoxyribonucleic acid, or DNA. To make a very complex story short, DNA is the code that allows living organisms to be what they are, whether plant, animal, bacteria, or fungi. DNA utilizes chemical compounds called *nucleotides* in specific sequences to form *genes*, and genes are the code that dictates what proteins a cell needs to form any one part of the body. We can use the analogy of a book to think about DNA. The nucleotides are the alphabet; although rather than 26 letters, in DNA there are only 4: *A, T, C*, and *G.* These four letters are paired into nucleotide bases, and they have to be strung together in specific ways to form words, or DNA.

When you're reading, each individual word has limited meaning by itself, but when words are put into sentences, and sentences are strung together to form paragraphs, much greater meaning emerges. DNA's sentences and paragraphs are genes. Together, the paragraphs in a book tell a complete story, in much the same way that genes are responsible for making up an organism. The full complement of genes in any organism is referred to as its *genome.*

When cells in any organism need to grow or repair themselves, they undergo a process called mitosis. During mitosis, the DNA in the cell divides and then remakes itself whole so that each new cell is an exact copy of the original. However, that process is not perfect. Even in a healthy body, there is an error in 1 in every approximately 100,000 nucleotides copied. While there are mechanisms in the cell to fix DNA damage, not everything is repairable.

As a body ages, the error rate of DNA replication tends to increase. When these errors begin to pile up, we wind up with dysfunctional or nonfunctional genes. This can lead to cells being unable to create the necessary proteins to maintain health or even to their becoming cancerous. The inability to replicate the genome with high fidelity (accuracy) is known as *genomic instability*.

Aging and other internal processes, however, are not the only causes of genomic instability. External factors can also play a role. Radiation from sources such as X-rays, prolonged sun exposure, and radon are known to cause genomic instability. While the mechanisms are somewhat different for each, the ionizing radiation from these sources causes breaks in DNA that can lead to nonfunctional genes or mutations of genes. Similarly, chemicals such as air and water pollutants (carbon monoxide, lead, particulates, agricultural by-products, and so forth), smoke (cigarette or otherwise), and certain drugs can also lead to genomic instability and altered DNA methylation (which, as will be explained in the "Epigenetic Age" section on page 46, is a critical part of *epigenetics*, or which genes get expressed).

Interestingly, research into the genomes of people who are over 100 years old shows that they have an increased ability to repair damaged DNA. Studies are underway to better understand exactly how this works, but it seems clear genetics, diet, and lifestyle all play a role. While there isn't much you and your cat can do about the genes you are born with, diet and lifestyle are factors completely within your control, and we'll take a look at that in Chapters 3 and 4.

Telomere Attrition

Genomic instability is not the only facet of DNA replication that can affect aging. The second hallmark of aging, *telomere attrition*, represents another hurdle standing in the way of your cat's ability to generate new cells when they are needed to maintain optimal health.

Chromosomes are the entirety of the genome. Essentially, they are strands of DNA that are wound up very tightly to make them compact enough to fit in the cell nucleus. Each chromosome is paired, as one copy comes from Mom and one from Dad. Cats have 38 chromosomes (19 pairs). For reference, humans have 46 chromosomes (23 pairs). Telomeres are "caps" at the ends of chromosomes. They serve to protect them from fraying or becoming damaged. They also prevent the ends of the DNA from sticking to other strands. DNA is "sticky" because the nucleotides are designed to form long strands and ultimately chromosomes. What we don't want is the end of one chromosome attaching itself to the end of another. This would prevent the cell from replicating and expressing genes—a catastrophic result.

Telomeres are required for DNA to replicate, and careful study has shown that over time and repeated cell divisions, they become shorter. This shortening is due to decreased activity of telomerase, the enzyme that helps them maintain their length. When they get too short, it becomes very difficult for cells to divide and the body is unable to repair itself. As we have all experienced, older cats (not to mention people) do not heal or recover as well or as quickly as they did when they were younger. One of the reasons for this is the inability to replicate cells due to shortened telomeres.

Shortened telomeres are not only a result of aging but can also be due to a lack of the telomerase enzyme. While telomerase deficiency and aging are not synonymous, the result of the deficiency—an inability to maintain telomere length, subsequently leading to cellular dysfunction—illuminates the importance of telomeres to health and longevity. In humans, telomerase deficiency is associated with early onset of diseases such as pulmonary fibrosis (scarring of the lungs due to a failure to create normal lung tissue) and aplastic anemia (inability to make new red blood cells). In animal models, telomerase deficiency leads to cellular senescence (another of the 14 hallmarks) and accelerated aging. There is—as always—balance in the body. Maintaining long telomeres is great in that they allow cells to effectively replicate to create new tissues and keep the body healthy. In the wrong cells, however, long telomeres can lead to unregulated cellular replication, which may indicate cancer.

Given this information, one could logically assume telomere length could be used as a measure of aging. While it has been used in precisely this way for years, recent studies do cast some doubt on telomere length as a biomarker for age. In other words, maintaining long telomeres is not directly predictive of a long life span. That said, there is still significant value in measuring telomere length within the larger picture of aging and longevity. We will discuss this as a diagnostic test and its applications in Chapter 2.

Epigenetic Alterations

Every individual's genome is unique to them, with the exception of identical twins, who share a genome. (Kittens in the same litter are rarely, if ever, identical twins. They may look the same, but they are fraternal twins and do not share a common genome.) From the moment of fertilization, the genome of that individual is set in stone. Nothing in the natural world can change it other than errors in DNA replication.

If the essentially immutable genome was the whole "health and longevity" story, many individuals would be in trouble. It is quite common for cats to carry genes that predispose them to degenerative conditions and even disease like cancer. But your cat's genome is not their destiny.

Think of the genome as an actor's script. Although there are specific words in the script, the actor may take some creative license, choosing how to emphasize certain phrases or even skipping some altogether. The same thing occurs in your cat's body. The body decides which genes to express and which to keep silent. This aggregate of expressed and unexpressed genes is referred to as the *epigenome*, or *epigenetics*. Unlike the genome, the epigenome changes over time. These changes can be due to nutrition, supplementation, exposure to toxins, the aging process, and so on. So, while we can't change your cat's genome, we can affect epigenetics, and epigenetics ultimately controls which genes are and aren't expressed in the body. One of the goals we're trying to accomplish in the quest for longevity for cats is finding ways to maintain an epigenetic profile that looks like that of a young, healthy cat, regardless of how chronologically old they are.

Many factors influence a body's specific expression of genes, but we're going to focus on DNA methylation. It turns out that DNA isn't really just a long string of nucleotide bases. Other molecules and chemical compounds are frequently bound to DNA, and these compounds often have impacts on gene expression (that is, epigenetics). Methyl groups, which are nothing more than a carbon atom with three hydrogen atoms attached, frequently bind to specific areas on DNA. DNA methylation can be used as a marker of epigenetic age through tests called *DNA methylation clocks.*[5] Unlike your cat's chronological age, DNA methylation age can be reversed to a certain extent through specific therapies. We will discuss methylation clocks and their value to longevity science in Chapter 2. Suffice it to say that while DNA methylation age is not a reliable predictor of life span, it is a highly effective tool to quantify the efficacy of longevity-focused therapies.

Loss of Proteostasis

Quick refresher: DNA codes for genes (the genome), and there are various mechanisms that regulate which genes in the genome are expressed (the epigenome). The epigenome codes for the formation of specific proteins, which serve an incredibly wide variety of purposes encompassing just about all functions in the body, from the immune system to how food is metabolized, and so forth. This spectrum of proteins created by your cat's body is known as the *proteome.*

You can think of proteins as intricately folded origami. One piece of paper can be folded infinite ways to achieve a variety of animals and shapes, but if you want a crane, it has to be folded in one specific way. Similarly, proteins must be folded correctly to be functional. Misfolded proteins lead to disruption of the body's ability to maintain health, and in humans, their buildup is associated with aging and age-related conditions like Alzheimer's, Parkinson's, and cataracts. Not surprisingly, the body has developed ways to either refold misfolded proteins to make them functional again or break them apart and recycle their components to make new proteins. The ability of the body to maintain proper folding of proteins is known as *proteostasis*, and improving proteostasis has been shown to delay conditions associated with aging. We will discuss how to support this process in our cats in upcoming chapters.

Deregulated Nutrient Sensing

Food, along with water and oxygen, provides the essential building blocks to grow, repair, and maintain body systems. In addition to serving as a substrate for these processes, food—its presence or absence—is responsible for a cascade of biochemical interactions.

Some studies show evidence that a reduced-calorie diet has effects on the body that can boost longevity through a variety of mechanisms, including promoting autophagy, decreasing cellular senescence, and increasing insulin sensitivity.[6] All of these things allow the body to function more like a young, healthy body rather than an aging one. Some folks have taken this information and run with it by severely restricting their own calorie intake in the hopes of living longer. The reality? Though calorie restriction plays a role, you have already seen that aging is affected by multiple biological processes, and therefore there's never going to be a "do this one thing" solution. Using calorie restriction as a standalone means of promoting longevity only results in a really, really hungry cat.

Instead, examining what happens when we restrict calories can bring the picture of longevity for cats into clearer focus. The term *nutrient sensing* refers to the body's biochemical response to food. For example, when your cat eats, it triggers the release of compounds such as growth hormone, insulin, and insulin-like growth factor. All these compounds assist in properly assimilating the consumed nutrients so the body can grow and maintain itself. However, cellular growth and metabolism also lead to cellular damage and, subsequently, aging.

Deregulated nutrient sensing refers to the state where the body is not responding appropriately to cycles of eating and not eating, is unable to remain in balance, and ages as a result. While the balance of nutrient sensing is affected by many factors, I want to introduce three useful proteins that we will be targeting when we discuss treatment options to promote longevity in your cat.

First, *mammalian target of rapamycin* (mTOR) is a protein that encourages the crucial processes of cell growth and repair.[7] The presence of this protein increases as your cat eats and exercises. But too much mTOR is implicated in a variety of aging pathways as well as an increase in cancer risk. In short, you want mTOR to be "on" some of the time but not too much of the time.

Then, the counterbalances to mTOR are *activated protein kinases* (AMPK), which are triggered by calorie restriction and exercise, and *sirtuins*, a group of proteins that can be activated by fasting as well as certain foods such as green tea, kale, and olive oil. Where mTOR builds things up through cellular growth and proliferation, AMPK breaks things down and helps rid the body of old, damaged, or otherwise malfunctioning cells. Sirtuins are similar, although they also play a role in repairing and stabilizing DNA damage. This is critical because all that old and damaged material promotes aging. Think of it this way: The house or apartment you live in needs periodic maintenance. Things become damaged—wood rots, roofs leak, and so on. That damaged material must be removed (AMPK) before it can be replaced with new materials (mTOR). You can't repair the house without removing the damaged material first, but neither can you live in the house with all the damaged items removed but not repaired. The key to longevity is creating and maintaining balance between building up and breaking down.

Mitochondrial Dysfunction

Mitochondria might be a term you remember from high-school biology, where it is often termed the "powerhouse of the cell." Mitochondria are the structures inside cells that, through a series of chemical processes, produce a compound called ATP that provides the necessary energy for the cell to conduct its business.

One fun fact you might not have learned in bio class: Millions of years ago mitochondria were free-living bacteria that, over time, evolved into a symbiotic relationship inside other cells. Although they are now most decidedly part of the cell, mitochondria retain their own DNA that is separate and distinct from the DNA that makes up chromosomes in the cell's nucleus. While the DNA in the nucleus of your cat's cells is a combination from Mom and Dad, mitochondrial DNA is directly inherited only from the mother. Admit it—biology is kind of cool.

You don't need a Ph.D. to recognize that if the power generators in cells aren't functioning well, there are going to be problems. Specifically, the problem is a lack of ATP, which means cellular systems can't operate at their best. Mitochondrial dysfunction can be caused by genetic factors as well as exposure to certain toxins, and the resultant lack of energy leads to cellular dysfunction and damage, potentially cancer, and—yes—aging.

Cellular Senescence

There are a lot of things that can go wrong with a cell. After all, these microscopic structures are an incredibly complex array of intracellular components, moving parts, and chemical interactions. Many of the previous hallmarks of aging cover some of the ways cells can get into trouble.

As if this isn't enough, cells can become damaged due to toxins, infection, or trauma.

Cells have a variety of tools at their disposal to repair DNA, adjust epigenetics, and fix or recycle proteins to maintain proteostasis. But what happens when the cell is beyond repair? When cells get to the point of no return regarding loss of function, they can become *senescent* and are sometimes referred to as "ghost cells." Senescence means the cell is still living, but it no longer carries out many of the metabolic functions it was originally designed for. The final result of the various hallmarks of aging is often an overabundance of senescent cells.

Cellular senescence is good news and bad news (here is that balance thing again). The good news is that when the damaged cell shuts down, it is unable to reproduce and create more damaged cells that could transform into cancer. So, keeping these cells quiet can be a very good thing. All bodies, young and old, have some senescent cells, although as the body ages, it accumulates more. The number of senescent cells in a body is referred to as its "senescent cell burden." And here comes the bad news: As these cells accumulate, they can lead to problems such as decreased tissue function, inflammation, and stem cell exhaustion (another of the hallmarks). These cells may also secrete chemical compounds that promote inflammation or damage in adjacent cells. As a result, senescent cells may stimulate neighboring cells to convert to a senescent state as well, further reducing the number of functional cells in the body.

As the body ages and loses its regenerative capacity due to genomic instability, telomere attrition, cellular senescence, and so on, fewer and fewer functioning cells remain. Over time, this leads to decreased function of the body as a whole. We will discuss measuring senescent cell burden as a tool for longevity therapies in Chapter 2.

Stem Cell Exhaustion

So far, we have covered many of the ways cells make new cells and how they can repair themselves or shut down if they are irrevocably broken. Beyond these mechanisms, the body has another method for creating new cells and new tissues, one that I am sure you have heard of: *stem cells.*

Stem cells are special because they can do something no others can: transform themselves into different types of cells. What we call fully differentiated cells have a very specific function. Take a heart cell as an example. In this case, heart cells make up the tissues that allow the heart to beat. A heart cell cannot suddenly be transformed into a kidney cell; there is no mechanism in the body to do this. Stem cells, sometimes called *progenitor cells,* are considered undifferentiated because they have the ability to become other, more specialized cells, such as heart or kidney cells. Just as an unsculpted block of clay has the potential to be transformed into an endless variety of vases, sculptures, or spoon rests, so too do stem cells have the ability to become more specific and specialized, such as heart, kidney, or bone cells.

You have undoubtedly heard about stem cell therapy, where stem cells are administered to a patient to encourage the healing of an illness or injury. Stem cell therapy has been used for years in veterinary medicine to treat arthritis in cats. The stem cells are injected into an affected joint (or injected intravenously) and will transform themselves into cartilage and other cell types that help support and repair the damage. This therapy is a big piece of a field called *regenerative medicine.*

A loss of viable stem cells is a big part of aging. The body can create new stem cells through certain supplements, some pharmaceuticals, and nutritional strategies, although generally they decline with age, as well as due to poor nutrition, toxin exposure, and other factors. On the whole, however, the older your cat gets, the fewer stem cells they have, and thus the less their body is able to build and repair tissues and maintain a healthy immune system. When a cat's body reaches the point where damage and dysfunction is outpacing its repair mechanisms and reserve of stem cells, the body begins to decline and display signs of aging.

Altered Intercellular Communication

Did you know cells in the body talk to one another? Communication between cells is actually a crucial method to maintain coordinated functioning throughout the body. The previous eight hallmarks of aging we have discussed all involve things that individual cells are doing. This ninth hallmark is about changes in communication between cells.

When we refer to *intercellular communication*, we are mostly talking about chemical signaling—such as from hormones, cytokines, and other compounds—although neuronal (electrical) communication happens as well. When cells lose the ability to communicate, they concurrently lose their ability to respond to the needs of the body.

As previously mentioned, as the body ages, the increasing population of senescent cells secrete compounds that signal neighboring cells to become senescent as well. This is sometimes referred to as *contagious aging* and is a type of altered intercellular communication. Whereas originally cellular senescence was caused by irreparable damage to a cell, thanks to secretory senescent cells, functioning cells are now being recruited too.

In upcoming chapters, we will discuss how intercellular communication can be improved through the use of nutrition, supplementation, and pharmaceuticals.

Compromised Autophagy

When your cat has not eaten for a period of time, different biochemical pathways are set in motion that promote a process called *autophagy.* Since new nutrients aren't coming in, the body has to work with what it's got, and damaged cells are consumed and recycled. Ultimately, there are biological benefits and costs to both eating and not eating. In order to maintain health and optimal function, the body needs to be able to create and build new cells and tissues. Everything in the body has a life span, however, and there are ways of cleaning up old and damaged cells in order to replace them with new and better-functioning ones. Promoting good health and longevity relies on an appropriate balance.

The process of autophagy, by which the body consumes parts of itself, may sound a little gross, but I assure you, it is absolutely necessary for all living beings. Consider it this way . . . if you have a loaf of old, moldy bread at home and you buy a new, fresh loaf, would you put the new loaf right next to the moldy one? Clearly you would not, because your new bread is going to get moldy much sooner than it would have had you disposed of the old bread first. With autophagy, your cat's body disposes of old and damaged cells by consuming them. This way, they can't have negative effects on neighboring, healthy cells.

As one of the more recently described hallmarks of aging, compromised autophagy was previously categorized as part of the "deregulated nutrient sensing" hallmark. Autophagy directly affects most of the other hallmarks of aging, because the cells being consumed are dysfunctional, which can lead to instability and cellular senescence that can cause aging and disease. Remember, the goal of longevity on a cellular level is to maintain the body's cells in a healthy, optimally functioning state. When a cell is no longer able to serve its function, it should be removed to make room for new, healthy cells.

Microbiome Disturbance

The *microbiome* describes the population of bacteria living in the gastrointestinal tract, or gut, of cats, people, and so forth. The fact that a healthy microbiome is critical to an individual's general health is something we have known for a long time. Recently, however, the microbiome has been directly linked to longevity and healthy aging through changes in the structural integrity of the GI tract, brain function, and levels of inflammation.[8]

We will discuss the microbiome in greater detail in upcoming chapters. For now, realize that the health of the microbes living in your kitty's gut is directly related to how long and how well they are likely to live. We have to take care of those little guys!

Altered Mechanical Properties

Imagine a bucket of water balloons, where the bucket itself is full of water so the balloons are kind of suspended inside. This is how we used to think of cells and the environment they live in. The truth, not surprisingly, is quite a bit more complex. There are actually scaffoldlike structures both within and between the cells that create form and provide proteins and other components with the ability to move around. These structures make up kind of a highway system, allowing the transport of compounds from one area of a cell to another or from one cell to another. In addition, some cells, such as white blood cells, need to move around in order to keep the body healthy. Just like when a bridge is out and you have to drive an hour out of your way to get home, when this cellular infrastructure becomes disrupted, the body is not able to operate optimally, which in turn leads to dysfunction and aging. The study of these mechanical functions is known as "mechanobiology," and while it is relatively new, it shows a lot of promise in the field of longevity science.

Splicing Dysregulation

We have previously discussed how errors in DNA (genomic instability) and altered structure of DNA (epigenetic alterations) contribute to aging. We also discussed loss of proteostasis, meaning proteins are "misfolded," leading to nonfunctional or abnormally functioning proteins. Another closely related factor is dysregulation of RNA. While DNA holds the "master genetic code," RNA is the "middleman" who reads the DNA and ultimately creates the proteins that the DNA codes for. When changes arise in RNA, splicing dysregulation occurs, and the integrity of the proteins that are formed is compromised, which can lead to protein dysfunction, disease, and aging.

Inflammation

One of the most prominent features of aging is the increase in inflammation throughout the body. This process, sometimes called *inflammaging*, is caused by tissue damage, immune system dysfunction, an inability to "clean up" damaged or senescent cells, pro-inflammatory secretions from senescent cells, and other factors. In short, there are a lot of causes of chronic inflammation, but what they have in common is furthering cellular damage and preventing cells from being able to appropriately communicate. While inflammation has long been known to be a contributor to aging, it was previously categorized within "altered intercellular communication." Given how prominent a role inflammation plays in the aging process, the scientific community has decided it warrants being considered a hallmark of aging on its own.

UNDERSTANDING THE ROOT CAUSE

When I was in veterinary school, my professors were quick to correct students who implied that a patient's condition was due to their age. "Age is not a disease," they would say. *Merriam-Webster* defines *disease* as "a condition of the living animal or plant body or of one of its parts that impairs normal functioning and is typically manifested by distinguishing signs and symptoms."[9] Based on this definition and what you now understand about the 14 hallmarks of aging, what do you think? Is aging a disease?

If it isn't, then we accept it as an inevitability and do little or nothing to stop it. Conversely, if it is a disease, we can approach treating and curing it like we do any other medical condition. First, we find out what causes it—the 14 hallmarks are an excellent foundation for this. Once we understand the underlying causes, we can set about the task of finding ways to prevent, treat, or at least limit the progression of this disease that affects every living thing on the planet. This is the basis of modern longevity science. So, how do we combat aging? More specifically, how do we approach maintaining health and youthful vigor for far longer than is currently considered normal?

One of the most critical steps in the quest for longevity is a step that, unfortunately, isn't taken often enough in the field of medicine. Each patient needs to be evaluated and treated as an individual. Yes, there are some through lines with medicine and longevity science. For example, it is important to keep inflammation in check in all cats. That said, each individual has their own strengths and weaknesses based on both internal factors (like the epigenome) and external factors (like exposure to environmental toxins). One cat may be prone to kidney disease based on their genetics or environmental factors, whereas another may be more at risk for arthritis.

Allopathic medicine tends to take a two-dimensional view when it comes to treatment. Physicians and veterinarians are taught to treat a diagnosis. They rarely discuss the underpinnings of the diagnosis. What genetic, environmental, or other variables led to the cat developing the condition? Although it may sound completely obvious, this is just not how doctors are trained. Allopathic medicine in general is geared toward treating the symptoms of disease without gaining an understanding of how to address the root cause. Granted, some of this is a function of doctors being overworked and not having the time to do a deep dive into each individual patient. In a more fundamental sense, however, allopathic medicine has evolved into a paradigm that doesn't spend a lot of time on prevention. While there are pharmaceutical interventions we will discuss within the context of longevity medicine, a lot of what we will talk about are preventive measures that don't generate a lot of revenue for either doctors or the pharmaceutical industry. And, if we are having an honest discussion here, the direction the medical profession takes is heavily influenced by the money behind Big Pharma.

To combat aging, we have to look at methods of testing, or quantifying, the processes that cause it, as well as metrics by which we can measure how a cat is aging in terms of their unique body. We can use these diagnostic tests to determine what specific areas each individual cat may need help with. The treatments may look like diet or nutritional changes, supplements, pharmaceuticals, and even interventional medical procedures. It all depends on what the individual needs.

A friend and colleague, Jeffrey Gladden, M.D., is one of the world's leading physicians in performance and antiaging medicine (for humans). He does extensive testing for his patients and then designs customized treatment protocols to improve their health and longevity. Because of the cutting-edge and constantly evolving nature of the science of aging, he is fond of saying, "We shouldn't be married to the answers; we should be married to the questions." This is a profound statement. Doctors are trained to seek answers, but the truth—as so often is the case in life—is only found after you ask the right questions.

Not asking the right questions is sometimes a function of a doctor pursuing an incorrect diagnostic or treatment pathway. I see kitties in my office all the time for chronic gastrointestinal problems. They are frequently diagnosed with inflammatory bowel disease, or IBD. The thing about IBD is that even though most veterinarians consider this a "disease," it really doesn't explain *why* there is inflammation, only that there *is* inflammation.

Not long ago, a cat named Molly was brought in for chronic diarrhea and weight loss. She had received an extensive workup—including bloodwork, ultrasounds, and intestinal biopsies—and the diagnosis was IBD. She was being treated with antibiotics, steroids, and prescription diets, which were only partially controlling the symptoms, and her owner was very concerned about the long-term effects these medications would have. In this case, the "right question" was "What is she eating that is causing her to have inflammation?" Food-sensitivity testing revealed she had a severe inflammatory response to several things she was eating. Once we removed them from her diet and supported her with probiotics and other natural supplements, Molly's IBD resolved in a few months, without the need for pharmaceuticals and prescription diets.

When it comes to longevity, however, not asking the right questions is more frequently an issue of doctors not knowing what questions to ask. When my professor said, "Age is not a disease," what he was really saying was "Don't ask about the specific pathways that cause aging and how we can intervene." It's not that my professor was closed-minded . . . that is how he was taught and how all doctors are taught. The current paradigm of Western medicine is that aging is an inevitability. We can try to treat the cancer, the heart disease, the kidney failure, and so on but not the underpinnings of why the body breaks down as we (and our pets) age. The questions that longevity science is asking are the questions that are going to allow us to "turn the corner" and prevent, or reverse, aging. Instead of treating the symptoms of aging (cancer, organ disease, and so forth), we will learn to prevent and treat the processes that lead to the diseases (symptoms) that ultimately end with bodily decline and death. These are the "answers" we seek. We, meaning modern medicine, must reframe our questions to get to the root cause of aging and not merely treat symptoms.

* * *

You now have a foundational understanding of many of the factors that cause the body to age and deteriorate. In truth, there are more than 14, and we will touch on a few others throughout our journey. From a treatment perspective, there are also many approaches to promote longevity because, as you have seen, aging is not caused by one single issue. We have to address as many of the hallmarks of aging as we can if we hope to achieve success, and the key is in maintaining balance in the body.

We will explore how to leverage nutrition, exercise, integrative medicine, specific supplements, therapies, and regenerative medicine. Equally important is a discussion of what you should avoid. And because the field of longevity science is expanding and making new discoveries all the time, we will discuss research and breakthroughs that point to what will become available in the near future to allow your cat to live an even longer and healthier life! In the next chapter we'll take a look at some of the diagnostic tests that can not only determine any potential problems in your cat but also help you measure how well certain interventions are working.

The Hallmarks of Aging*

*Reprinted from *Cell,* Volume 153/Issue 6, Carlos López-Otín, Maria A. Blasco, Linda Partridge, Manuel Serrano, and Guido Kroemer, "The Hallmarks of Aging," pages 1194–1217, copyright 2013, with permission from Elsevier.

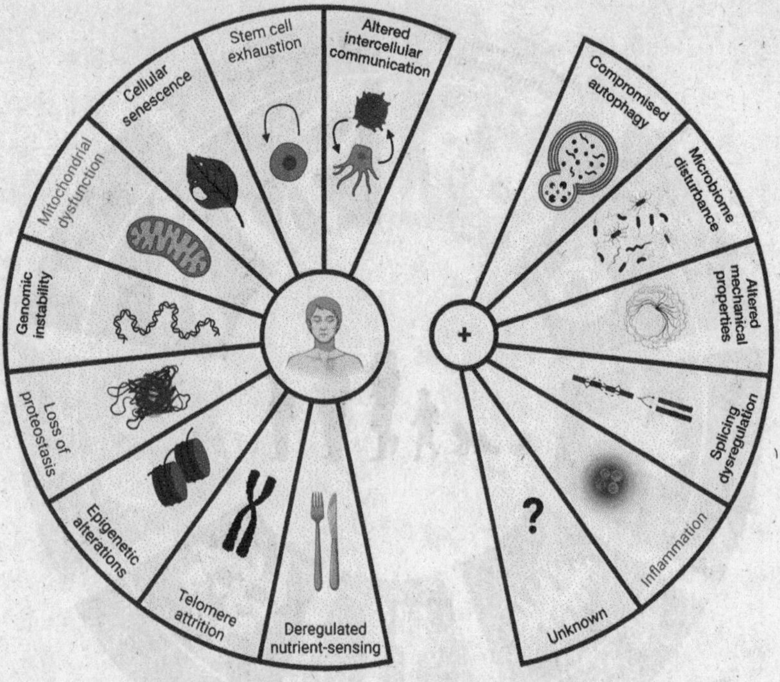

New Hallmarks of Ageing*

---

* © 2022 Schmauck-Medina et al. (CC by 3.0)
Schmauck-Medina T, Molière A, Lautrup S, Zhang J, Chlopicki S, Madsen HB, Cao S, Soendenbroe C, Mansell E, Vestergaard MB, Li Z, Shiloh Y, Opresko PL, Egly JM, Kirkwood T, Verdin E, Bohr VA, Cox LS; Stevnsner T, Rasmussen LJ, Fang EF. "New hallmarks of ageing: a 2022 Copenhagen ageing meeting summary." *Aging* (Albany NY). 2022 Aug 29;14(16):6829-6839. doi: 10.18632/aging.204248. Epub 2022 Aug 29. PMID: 36040386; PMCID: PMC9467401.

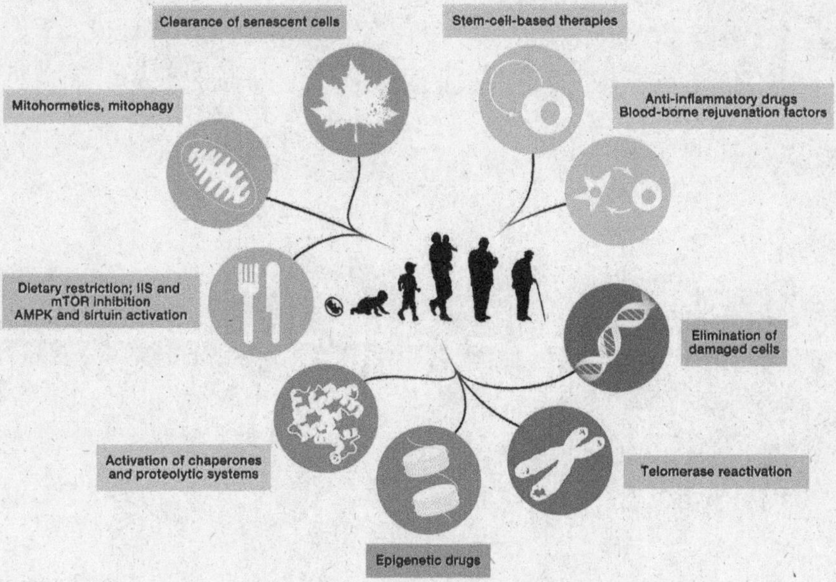

Interventions That Might Extend Human Healthspan*

* Reprinted from *Cell*, Volume 153/Issue 6, Carlos López-Otín, Maria A. Blasco, Linda Partridge, Manuel Serrano, and Guido Kroemer, "The Hallmarks of Aging," pages 1194–1217, copyright 2013, with permission from Elsevier.

CHAPTER 2

DIAGNOSTIC TESTING

Ponce de León and all those who came before and after him failed in the quest for immortality because they weren't asking the right questions. They didn't have the understanding we now do of what aging really is. It turns out that "Could someone please direct me to the magic fountain of immortality?" is not going to solve the longevity puzzle. That said, given what he had to work with at the time, it was about as good a question as any.

Only recently has the scientific community begun to uncover the means with which to ask the right questions and thus uncover the right answers. After all, the human genome was fully mapped only in 2003, and almost everything we are discussing in this book has been discovered in the last 20 years.[1] With the foundation of the 14 hallmarks that contribute to aging, the next logical question is: What can we do with this knowledge? In other words, how do we leverage the information to help our cats live longer, healthier lives?

As we have discussed, aging is not caused by one single issue. It happens because of a compilation of many processes in the body that, over time, lead to diminished ability to heal and regenerate tissues, decreased immune system function, and increased incidence of cancer. While the susceptibility to disease, such as cancer, and other degenerative processes is a challenge all cats face, the specifics of their health strengths and weaknesses vary from one cat to the next due to their individual genome. This is where diagnostic testing becomes part of the longevity story.

The newness of understanding how the genome, epigenome, proteome, and so on affect aging is the reason why the discussion of longevity is so fascinating right now. For the first time in human history, we are uncovering the processes that cause aging and finding ways to measure them. And if you can measure them, then you can look for treatments that make the measurements better and, subsequently, keep your cat youthful and healthy. Remember, testing is not only about finding out what your cat is susceptible to but also about monitoring their progress once aging interventions (diet, supplements, medications, and treatments) have begun, so we know what is working and how to make our cats physiologically younger. In this chapter we'll take a look at some current diagnostic-testing options, such as blood-count and chemistry panels; genetic testing; and screening for specific medical conditions, food sensitivities, and overall gut health so that you can make the best health decisions for your individual cat. I'll also explain some of the exciting new tests for humans (and some dogs), like measuring oxidative stress or detecting cancer, so that you can be prepared to utilize them when they become available for cats in the near future.

TESTING OPTIONS FOR TODAY

Until recently, there were few, if any, diagnostic tests that would allow us to even begin to ask the critical questions surrounding aging. If I had written this book 10—or even 5—years ago, the number of available options for diagnostic testing would be a fraction of what they are now. And 10 years from now? Oh boy—wait until you see what is coming!

Because of the rapidly changing landscape of available diagnostic testing related to aging, I've divided this chapter between discussing what testing is available for your cat right now and what is coming in the near future: the next 5 or 10 years. Given the rapidity with which the science is progressing, it may be even sooner than that.

The vast majority of diagnostic testing in veterinary medicine in the United States is done through two labs, IDEXX and Antech. Most of the more longevity-focused testing is performed by other, smaller laboratories that are not necessarily what the veterinary profession might describe as mainstream. To be clear, these smaller labs are highly qualified and provide reliable and actionable results for those who understand how to interpret them. Not being "mainstream" in this context means that most veterinarians are probably not aware of them, because they utilize only IDEXX or Antech for lab services. As we move through the tests, I'll provide you with the names of the laboratories offering them so you can discuss them with your veterinarian. Hopefully, if they are open-minded, they will be willing to explore some new avenues of diagnosis and ultimately treatment. I also provide a brief explanation of what the test is for as well as how it fits into the longevity puzzle. Wherever possible, I'll let you know which of the hallmarks of aging apply to that specific test.

Standard Blood Panels

The place to begin our discussion of the diagnostic options currently available to your cat is with the routine blood panels your veterinarian runs every day. The cornerstone of laboratory screening in veterinary (and human) medicine is the complete blood count (CBC) and chemistry panel. These tests are the primary means by which modern medicine evaluates the health of a patient, and many medical conditions can be diagnosed and monitored through this type of screening. It is important to understand what these tests can and cannot tell us about your cat's health, as there are lots of misconceptions among pet owners about what can be determined from a standard blood panel.

Blood is composed of cells suspended in liquid. The cells—red blood cells, white blood cells, and platelets—are evaluated by the CBC. Changes in number can indicate significant medical problems like anemia, infection, inflammation, and autoimmune disease, among others. Serum, on the other hand, is the liquid component of the blood and is evaluated in a chemistry panel. Chem panels are able to look at parameters of organ function such as those of the liver and kidneys as well as hydration, electrolytes, blood proteins, fats, and so on. Changes in these values can indicate poor organ function, endocrine (hormonal) imbalances, dehydration, and other disease processes. Beyond standard blood chemistries, your veterinarian has access to hundreds of other tests used to diagnose specific issues, such as abnormalities in thyroid function, screening for pancreatitis, indicators of heart disease, and so forth. The CBC and chemistry panel and the various other available ancillary tests are highly valuable diagnostic tools for your veterinarian to look at the overall health of your cat, and they should continue to be so.

As with every diagnostic test, there are limitations. While a "normal-looking" CBC and chemistry panel is a good indicator of health, it is not a measure of how old your cat is or how fast they are aging. In fact, veterinarians routinely see geriatric cats whose blood work looks fantastic, yet the cat is infirmed with age-related disease and may not have much time left. Perhaps the most glaring shortfall of a CBC and chemistry panel is its inability to diagnose nearly all cancers. Many people assume if their cat has cancer, it will show up in a routine blood test. But it almost never does. Unless we are talking about a cancer of the blood such as leukemia, most cats with cancer will have normal blood panels (but see more on cancer testing later in this chapter).

Getting back to the concept of asking the right questions, diagnostic testing is our means of asking the questions that will lead us to the answers to better health and longevity. A CBC, a chem panel, and the other tests often included in a routine workup ask specific questions that frequently provide valuable answers. While the information *is* valuable, we should not make the mistake of assuming there aren't a lot more questions to ask.

Genetic Testing

Recall that the sequence of DNA unique to every individual is called the genome. The genes in the DNA code for proteins that affect how the body functions. But not every gene in the DNA is transcribed into proteins. The spectrum of genes that are expressed is known as the epigenome. While treatments such as gene therapy will someday be able to change the genome of an organism, for our purposes, think of the genome as something largely written in stone. Your cat was born with their genome, and, barring errors in DNA replication, it will be the same throughout their life.

It is now possible to evaluate our cats for specific genetic markers that let us know what genes they have in their DNA. This is beneficial because some genes confer benefits to health and longevity, while others may predispose your cat to specific medical conditions. Understanding your cat's specific genetic markers can help us keep an eye out for specific problems they may be prone to. While the genome is written in stone, the epigenome is not. In other words, even though your cat may have a gene that has the potential to lead to problems, there may be things we can do to limit, or even prevent, its expression. Within the context of the hallmarks of aging, this fits into epigenetic alterations. If a deleterious gene is not being expressed, it can do no harm.

The most common commercial genetic-marker test for cats is from Basepaws. They offer a screening that can tell you the breed makeup of your cat; sequence their genome; and evaluate 65 genetic markers for disease, including hypertrophic cardiomyopathy (HCM), the most common form of heart disease in cats. They also have a test that looks for specific markers for dental disease in kitties.

As previously noted, just because a cat carries a gene for a disease does not mean they do, or ever will, have the disease. Since your cat's DNA is a combination of contributions from Mom and Dad, they have two copies of each gene, and the risk of disease has to do with the genes being the same (homozygous) or different (heterozygous) and if they are dominant or recessive.

In cases where symptoms suggest a specific medical condition but there is no definitive diagnosis, knowing if a cat carries a certain gene can be very helpful—for example, knowing if a cat is genetically predisposed to HCM. Frequently, kitties with HCM do not have a murmur, and they have no clinical signs until they either go into heart failure, develop a life-threatening condition called a saddle thrombus, or suddenly die with no warning. Kitties that have the HCM gene are not guaranteed to get the disease, but knowing that they carry it gives us the opportunity to monitor these cats more closely and begin treatment before problems arise.

In addition to confirming or ruling out a diagnosis, testing genetic markers allows us to know what the cat may be prone to in the future so we are aware of what to look out for. Also, for any cat breeders, it is critical to know what is in the parents' genetic makeup so they don't inadvertently breed cats likely to produce offspring with genetic diseases.

Biochemical Markers of Disease

Another lab that is running some exciting diagnostics for cats is VDI Laboratory. VDI has put together combinations of tests, many of which are not otherwise readily available, to screen for particular medical conditions in cats and dogs. Test panels include evaluation of vitamin levels and markers for inflammation, arthritis, and cancer. There are too many specific tests to discuss each one, although a few are worth highlighting, including vitamin D, magnesium, and thymidine kinase type 1 (TK1).

Chances are you are vitamin D deficient—most of us are. Unfortunately, the same is true for our cats. But unlike humans, cats do not synthesize vitamin D from sunlight. Their vitamin D comes from dietary sources only, and even though you may be feeding your cat an ideal diet (more on that in Chapter 3), they're probably still deficient. Easily 90 percent of the cats I have tested in my office who are not on a vitamin D supplement are deficient.

Vitamin D is incredibly important when it comes to aging. It promotes autophagy, or recycling of old or damaged cells. It also inhibits mitochondrial dysfunction; decreases oxidative stress and inflammation; and inhibits epigenetic alterations, genomic instability, and telomere shortening.[2] That's at least 5 of the 14 hallmarks of aging being affected by something as commonplace as vitamin D! Correcting vitamin D deficiency is as easy as sending a little blood to the lab for testing and then supplementing as indicated based on the cat's levels. Follow-up testing to monitor levels over time is always a good idea.

Another low-hanging fruit when it comes to longevity testing is magnesium levels. Magnesium plays a role in energy metabolism, cell proliferation, apoptosis (programmed cell death), oxidative stress, and inflammation.[3] Again, just like vitamin D, this mineral affects quite a few of the hallmarks of aging, and it is easy to supplement.

TK1 is an enzyme in cells that is involved with cell division. One of the characteristics of cancer is uncontrolled or unregulated cell division leading to tumor formation, so TK1 levels can become elevated when cancer is present.[4] Not surprisingly, the earlier cancer is diagnosed in cats, the more likely it is that treatment will be effective. Evaluating TK1 in cats can provide insight that allows for early intervention and a greater chance at a long, healthy life.

VDI runs a variety of panels geared toward patients who have particular medical issues. An appropriate panel, such as a GI panel, arthritis panel, or cancer panel, can be enormously valuable in addition to the CBC and chem panel your veterinarian will order as a routine health screen. Remember, the value here is not only in diagnosing a disease or a vitamin or mineral deficiency but also in being able to monitor your cat's progress after treatment has begun. All cats are individuals and respond to treatment differently. Understanding how *your* cat is responding will allow your veterinarian to tailor treatment to fit their needs.

Inflammation from Food

As I've touched upon, inflammation can have negative effects on intercellular communication, which contributes to aging. The lab Hemopet has a saliva-based test called NutriScan that measures antibodies, specifically IgA and IgM, and how they react to certain food ingredients.[5] This test gives you an idea of which foods your cat has a sensitivity to and will lead to inflammation in the gut. There are other food-sensitivity tests out there, some using saliva and others using blood. None of these tests are 100 percent accurate when it comes to determining the foods your cat is sensitive to, but in my experience, NutriScan is the most reliable food-sensitivity test available.

Clearly, the benefit of diagnostic testing is that it helps eliminate guesswork. I'm sorry to say that sometimes treatment decisions in medicine are "educated guesses," based on how other patients have historically responded to treatment. This is true regardless of whether we are talking about allergies, GI problems, cancer, or any number of other conditions. It is also true for both allopathic medicine and holistic care. When we can test for something specific, however, it allows us to take more direct and effective action.

In my office, it is an everyday occurrence for a pet owner to bring in an animal with a chronic condition where conventional medical treatment has failed. There are many reasons for this, but the most common is that the pet is diagnosed with a condition that has a lot of possible underlying causes. For example, I recently saw a kitty in my office named Socks who had chronic allergies that led to incessant scratching and licking. Socks was also frequently in a bad mood. The veterinarians who had previously treated Socks used medications and prescription diets to help, but these efforts met with only partial success, and every time the treatment was stopped, his allergies grew worse again.

Generally, people and animals have allergic reactions to something in their environment (dust, pollen, and the like), something they are eating, or both. While statistically environmental allergies are most common, food frequently plays a part. Given the extensive efforts that had already been made with Socks, I decided it would be a good idea to run a food-sensitivity test to see if this could be part of his problem. When the test came back, it was clear Socks had sensitivities to beef, chicken, lamb, and turkey. When I looked through his medical history, I found that even when Socks's diet had been changed in the past, he was always eating one of those four proteins. I converted him to a fresh, whole-food diet using pork as a protein, and within weeks he was feeling better. Interestingly, the more his skin improved, the friendlier and more loving Socks became. He was cranky because he didn't feel good. It was the diagnostic testing that allowed us to finally find the key to Socks getting better.

Microbiome

You may have heard about the relationship of gut health to overall health, and now you know disturbances in the microbiome are considered a hallmark of aging. This has a lot to do with the fact that 70 to 80 percent of the immune cells in your cat's (and your own) body are in the gastrointestinal tract.[6] An unhealthy microbiome leads to inflammation, poor nutrient absorption, and decreased mitochondrial function, which affect the function of the entire body. There is also a definitive link between gut health and brain health, known as the *gut–brain axis*. Thus, it will probably come as no surprise to you that the makeup of the bacterial population in the gut, known as the microbiome, plays a part in your cat's longevity. In humans, we already know that specific microbiome patterns are correlated with longevity.[7]

When it comes to our cats, there are two diagnostic labs available to evaluate their microbiome. Texas A&M University Veterinary School runs a test called a *dysbiosis index*, and AnimalBiome will run your cat's full microbiome. The A&M dysbiosis index measures specific bacteria in a stool sample and provides information regarding the health of your cat's microbiome. This test can be particularly valuable for cats with chronic gastrointestinal disease or, really, any kind of chronic illness. AnimalBiome's testing also looks at the spectrum of microflora (bacteria) in your cat's GI tract. In both cases, abnormalities in the microbiome can be a cause and a symptom of a host of issues affecting quality and quantity of life. So much of the immune system is in the gut that seemingly unrelated diseases, like allergies, autoimmune conditions, cognitive impairment, and others, may trace at least some of their origins to the microbiome. We will discuss ways to improve your cat's microbiome in Chapters 3 and 6.

TESTING OPTIONS FOR TOMORROW

There are likely more diagnostic tests focused on prolonging life span and health span than you might have thought. And, if I'm being honest, there are more available options than a general-practice veterinarian is likely to be currently utilizing. As fascinating and useful as this catalog of tests is, what is coming in the near future is even more exciting. Most of the diagnostics described in the upcoming section are already available for humans, which generally means they will become available for cats before too long. Even though research and testing for cats are in early stages for many of these, we can still use what we know about the affected body systems to consider and apply therapies that can increase longevity.

One note about the medical "establishment," be it human or veterinary, is that it is extremely slow to adopt new approaches to health care, especially when they run counter to long-held beliefs. The idea that aging and death are inevitable is about as deeply rooted a belief as there is in medical practice, and a large segment of the medical community will dismiss any concept suggesting otherwise as being outrageous and a fool's errand. Like everything else in medicine, however, what seems outlandish today will be accepted as mainstream tomorrow. For those of us who can see what is coming, there is no need to wait for the establishment to give us permission to help our cats live longer than ever.

Omics

A good way to look at forthcoming diagnostic options is to sequence or order them in the same way cellular function either contributes to healthy living or aging, depending on whether or not these systems are in proper working order. Ultimately, this sequencing is a measurable series of processes called *omics* that indicates how well a body is functioning and how its functions relate to either promoting or inhibiting the aging process. The progression of the five "omes" is: genome → epigenome → transcriptome → proteome → metabolome.

- As we discussed in Chapter 1, it all starts with your cat's DNA, also referred to as their **genome**.

- Not all of the genes in the DNA are expressed and transcribed into proteins. The spectrum of genes that are expressed at any given time is referred to as the **epigenome**. The expression of the genes is often referred to as epigenetics.
- In order for the epigenome to be expressed, DNA is transcribed into RNA, which is in turn translated into proteins. The full spectrum of what the cell is transcribing is called the **transcriptome**.
- The specific proteins created by the cell based on the transcriptome is called the **proteome**.
- All the proteins created by cells ultimately govern how the cells, and the whole body, function. The functioning of all the cells is referred to as their metabolism. Metabolic processes in the cell result in the formation of small molecules that can be measured, which gives us an idea of cellular activity and physiologic status. The aggregate of these small molecules is known as the **metabolome**.

Advanced Genome Testing

Earlier in this chapter, we discussed tests that look at portions of your cat's genome. Several private labs and universities are able to evaluate the genome and check for specific genetic markers that could indicate predisposition to specific diseases. These tests, however, examine only a tiny fraction of the entire genome.

The feline genome contains approximately 20,000 genes (the human genome contains 20,000 to 25,000). Interestingly, almost 16,000 of the feline genes are orthologs, meaning they share a common genetic ancestor with both humans and mice.[8] This is, of course, consistent with what we know about evolution. The genetic-marker tests we reviewed earlier look at 65 genes, so as you can see, most of your cat's genes are not currently being analyzed.

The truth is, no one knows what all those genes do, whether they are in your cat, yourself, a mouse, or a fruit fly. For a long time, researchers thought a lot of DNA was "junk DNA," meaning it didn't code for anything. Now it appears that scientists just didn't have a full understanding of all the functions DNA was responsible for. As time goes on, we will learn more about your cat's 20,000 genes, and you will eventually be able to run your cat's entire genome, just like you can your own. With this information, your cat's genetic tendencies will be greatly illuminated, and we will likely have the opportunity to strategically promote expression of beneficial genes and silence the ones that play a role in aging and disease—changing your cat's epigenetics. A little further down the road, gene therapy will become available to repair or replace genes that are disadvantageous to your cat's health.

The ability to change your cat's epigenetics is not far around the bend. As cats age, their gene expression changes, and that is a big part of aging. Remember, the epigenome is where it all starts as far as protein expression goes, and the process continues all the way down the cascade to the metabolome. Once we are able to fully evaluate the epigenome and then adjust it to reflect a younger cat, your kitty is going to be looking and acting their best for a very long time.

Omega Fatty Acids

In addition to vitamin D and magnesium, omega-3 fatty acids are another critical nutrient for all pets. These beneficial fats decrease inflammation, promote circulation, support neurologic function, and aid in digestion, along with conferring a host of other benefits. Omega fatty acids are found in marine lipids such as fish oil, krill oil, and algae oil. While omega fatty acids are also found in plant sources such as flaxseed oil, they are not particularly bioavailable compared to marine sources and, as such, supplements from these sources are not recommended for your cat. A recent study evaluating the effects of omega-3 fatty acids in humans found that a one percent increase in omega-3s in the blood correlated to an almost five-year increase in life span.[9] That's a similar life-span increase to a person quitting smoking.

In my office, we routinely test dogs for their omega fatty acid levels, and the large majority are deficient, even when they are consuming a good diet. The test kit for cats is not yet available, but it should be coming soon. Until we get there, adding some fish oil to your cat's bowl is an excellent longevity move. This is discussed more in Chapter 6.

Oxidative Stress

Undoubtedly, you have heard of antioxidants. They are popular in the supplement market for good reason. Antioxidants can help protect tissues from damage caused by oxidation. The body produces its own antioxidants, and in a perfect world, there is a balance (there's that word again) between oxidation and antioxidants. So, to be clear, oxidation is a vital process that helps rid the body of damaged or even cancerous cells. Problems, however, do occur when the level of oxidation is out of balance with the body's ability to counteract it. Excessive oxidation in the body is called *oxidative stress* and is, among other things, a cause of the aging hallmark mitochondrial dysfunction.[10]

Hemopet has developed a test, CellBIO, that measures levels of a compound called isoprostane in the saliva of dogs.[11] To make a long story short, isoprostane is produced when essential fatty acids (like omega-3s) undergo oxidative damage. Thus, isoprostane, and subsequently the CellBIO test, can be used as a measurement of oxidative stress and how it can improve over time when treated. This test is not currently available for cats, but it may be in the future.

Epigenetic Age

One feature of the epigenome that is very, very close to being realized is determining cats' epigenetic age. In Chapter 1, we briefly discussed DNA methylation clocks, which estimate age based on a blood sample. The real benefit here is, unlike chronological age, methylation age is reversible. That's right: certain therapies can actually make you or your cat appear younger based on their methylation patterns. In human medicine, DNA methylation clocks are being used to monitor responses to longevity therapies. The goal is to lower the patient's methylation age, and this is readily achievable with many different longevity interventions, ranging from diet and exercise to stem cell therapy. For all its usefulness, DNA methylation age is not directly correlated to life span. A similar test is being developed that is designed to be a specific predictor of life span. To say it another way, the test would tell you when you (or your cat) are likely to die based on your current health status. Depending on how you look at it, that could be a super useful tool or super scary. Appropriately, the name of this test is Grim Age.

DNA methylation clocks exist, although a feline version is not commercially available yet. Interestingly, the UCLA researcher who invented methylation clocks, Dr. Steve Horvath, has told me his dog clock is actually more accurate than the one he developed for humans. In addition to clocks for humans and dogs, a "pan-species" clock has been developed that should work for cats. The technology is here—it's just waiting for someone to commercialize it.

Transcriptome, Proteome, and Metabolome Analysis

Evaluating the transcriptome provides insight into what genes are expressed during different medical conditions and at different stages of your cat's life. This information will offer insight into medical conditions your cat may be susceptible to and, as such, may hint at therapeutic options for treatments that may eventually become available. Transcriptome analysis is currently available for human patients, so it is on its way to the veterinary world.

Evaluating the proteome and metabolome is a little further down the road than some of the other omics. Being able to evaluate these two "omes" in an organism (human, cat, or otherwise) will provide a clearer picture of exactly what proteins are being produced and metabolic function and health, respectively. These evaluations are largely in the research phase at this point, and it will likely be some time before they are commercially available for cats.

Is it really necessary to measure and monitor all five of the "omes" in the quest to promote longevity? We don't really know right now, but probably not. My prediction is that two or possibly three of them will prove to be useful predictive measures of both aging and efficacy of age-related therapies, but research is ongoing.

Telomeres

As the segments of DNA at the ends of the chromosomes, telomeres are vital to a cell's ability to replicate DNA and therefore create new cells. The older your cat gets, the shorter their telomeres become and the less able they are to repair and replace cells and tissues. Thus, aging accelerates. For a long time, as I mentioned before, it was presumed telomere length was a good prognostic indicator of longevity. It makes sense, right? Young people and animals have long telomeres and older ones have shorter telomeres, so the shorter the telomeres are, the more advanced the patient's age.

Well, science often has a few tricks up its sleeve, and current research would indicate measuring telomere length is not a great predictor of longevity.[12] The current feeling is that epigenetic age (measured by DNA methylation clocks) is more predictive, although it should be said that none of these diagnostics are rock-solid. There are trends but not absolutes, and there's no test available that will tell you how long you, or your cat, are going to live. All that said, given it is a measure of one of the hallmarks of aging, telomere length is still a useful parameter in the overall evaluation of health and longevity.

Telomere length is now commonly measured in humans who are proactive with longevity therapy. Telomeres control DNA replication, so understanding your telomere length can be a window into how able your body is to make new cells and repair itself. There are products on the market that are designed to help lengthen telomeres, so being able to measure them helps determine the efficacy of these products. A few companies are beginning to offer telomere-lengthening products and telomere testing for cats, although it hasn't hit its stride just yet. Though the diagnostics might not be available quite yet, you can still consider therapies to help keep your cat's telomeres looking young and healthy, which we'll discuss in Chapter 6.

Plasmalogens

Though the hallmarks we've discussed provide a great outline for discussion and research, there are factors beyond them that contribute to the aging process. More and more are being discovered, and this is why the quest for longevity is finally making actual progress after thousands of years. One factor that has come to light is *plasmalogens.*

Plasmalogens are components of all cellular membranes and are in particularly high concentration in the brain, heart, lungs, kidneys, and eyes. They appear to have several functions, including serving as a source of antioxidants (limiting oxidative stress) and omega fatty acids. Plasmalogens make up about 20 percent of the cell membrane, and their presence (or absence) has a substantial impact on cellular function.[13, 14]

Research indicates plasmalogen levels decline with age and are associated with diseases such as cardiac conditions, diabetes, cancer, dementia, Parkinson's, Alzheimer's, and multiple sclerosis in humans.[15] The bottom line is that decreasing levels of plasmalogens are correlated with a higher probability of dying. There is also some evidence to suggest decreasing levels are due to mitochondrial dysfunction, which brings us back to one of the original 14 hallmarks.[16, 17] Very little research into plasmalogens has been conducted in cats as of yet, although there is every reason to believe these compounds play just as critical a role in feline health and aging as they do in that of us humans. Plasmalogen testing is currently available in human medicine, and there are supplements to support plasmalogen levels in the body. We will discuss ways you can support your cat's plasmalogen levels in Chapter 6.

Senescent Cell Burden

Senescent cells are living but nonfunctional. All cats (and people) have some senescent cells, and they do serve a purpose. Specifically, they are associated with wound healing, immune system function, and suppression of cancer.[18] However, as your cat grows older, their senescent cell burden increases, which is a major contributor to aging. You may also recall that senescent cells frequently secrete compounds that recruit other cells to become senescent and further accelerate the aging process. The term for these cells is *senescence-associated secretory phenotype* (SASP). SASP can be measured and used to understand how a person (and ultimately, your kitty) is aging.[19] Supplements and medications that eliminate senescent cells are known as *senolytics*, and as you might expect, a lot of research is going into these. More about reducing your cat's senescent cell burden with senolytics can be found in Chapter 6.

Cancer

I mentioned earlier that one of the large drawbacks to blood tests is the inability to detect cancer. Since one in five cats will get cancer in their lifetime, this is a serious problem.[20] Given that a similar problem exists in human medicine, a lot of resources have been put forth to find a solution.

The liquid biopsy is the next big thing in cancer diagnostics. Generally, a biopsy is the removal of a piece of tissue for the purposes of analyzing it, usually to determine if it is cancerous. The problem with biopsies is they can be difficult, costly, and taxing on the body, as they require anesthesia, surgery, and recovery time. The other problem is that, in its earliest stages, cancer has no symptoms, meaning you don't have any indication a biopsy is necessary, much less what tissue you are supposed to collect, until the cancer is more advanced and potentially more dangerous. Liquid biopsy aims to fix this problem.

Technically not a real biopsy, the liquid biopsy is a blood sample that is analyzed for circulating tumor DNA (ctDNA). You see, when cancer is present, cancerous cells or pieces of cells break off and travel through the bloodstream. When whole cancer cells enter the blood, the cancer metastasizes (spreads). This test offers the opportunity to find cancer earlier than we otherwise would, as well as to monitor if a cancer patient is in remission.

While liquid biopsies are receiving a lot of focus and research dollars in human medicine, PetDx is the first company in the veterinary field to offer one for pets. While currently only available for dogs, this test is very exciting, because early diagnosis of cancer is the key to successful treatment. As with everything in life, however, the devil is in the details, and there are some shortcomings with the current technology.

In scientific terms, the accuracy of a test is measured by its sensitivity and specificity. *Sensitivity* refers to the likelihood a test will read positive when the sample is actually positive (in this case, detection of cancer). *Specificity* refers to the likelihood a test will read negative when the sample is negative. In other words, is it coming up with false positives in dogs that don't actually have cancer? The good news about the PetDx test is that in a published study, the specificity was found to be 98.5 percent—there are very few false-positive results, and a negative result is very likely to mean the dog does not have cancer. The not-so-good news is the sensitivity was 54.7 percent, meaning that cancer was actually detected in only a little more than half of the positive samples.[21]

In this case, the correctly diagnosed samples were almost exclusively from dogs with known cancer. (To be fair, the study also found cancer in four dogs who had not previously been diagnosed.) This matters because if the cancer is already diagnosable through more conventional means, the blood test isn't really all that valuable. The ideal for cancer diagnosis is at the earliest stages, before there is any detectable disease. Unfortunately, it doesn't look like the PetDx test is able to do that reliably just yet.

I expect availability of liquid-biopsy testing for cats will follow fairly closely behind the testing for dogs. Despite its current shortcomings, liquid biopsy is a very promising diagnostic test that likely will become a staple in both human and veterinary medicine once the sensitivity of the test improves significantly.

* * *

Diagnostic testing is an incredibly important tool in our quest for longevity for our pets. Most available tests, however, are accessible only through your veterinarian, and the reality is that while the information is valuable, testing alone is not going to make your cat live longer. Our next step is to discuss what you can do now to actually help your cat live a longer, healthier life. Certainly, we will explore high-tech and cutting-edge medicine, but some of the most effective longevity interventions are easy things you can do at home.

PART II

WHAT YOU CAN DO RIGHT NOW

CHAPTER 3

NUTRITION

I've got good news: some of the most effective longevity treatments you can implement for your cat are low-tech and easy to accomplish. When I talk with a cat owner about how to best care for their kitty, regardless of whether the cat is healthy or has a serious medical condition, the discussion always (and I mean *always*) begins with nutrition.

Think of nutrition as you might think of car maintenance. Your car runs on gas, oil, and various other fluids, and it will have optimal performance when the correct fluids are in it. What happens if you use the wrong kinds? Possibly the car will still run, but not as well as it should. It will also be far more prone to internal damage and breakdown. The same is true for a biological system like your cat, except biology is actually much more forgiving than a car.

As simple as it sounds, longevity begins with putting the right fuel in the biological machine that is your kitty. As it turns out, nutrition is actually a big part of the problem—and solution—when it comes to cats and longevity. When cats are fed the wrong fuel, over time it causes their bodies to age faster and develop more medical problems than they otherwise would. And because the body takes longer to break down than your car, by the time medical problems are apparent, they have likely been adversely affecting the cat for years and years. Reversing that damage can be difficult and sometimes impossible. This is why, ideally, you should start your pet on an optimal diet from day one, or at least as soon as possible. In this chapter I will outline the most important nutrients, vitamins, and minerals to look for in food; which type of food preparation is best; and the right amount to feed your cat.

FROM WILD CATS TO HOUSE CATS

When we think about ideal nutrition for cats, it is best to start with an understanding of where your kitty comes from. Depending on what paper you read, cats have been domesticated for somewhere between 10,000 and 12,000 years.[1] It all started with the wild cat, *Felis sylvestris*, who was present during the development of agricultural villages in the Fertile Crescent, in the modern-day Middle East. Stable agriculture and grain storage would have led to a population explosion of small mammals like mice and rats, a ready-made food supply for cats. Over a very, very long time, there was an unintentional selection for specific traits in the wild cats. The cats who were less afraid or less aggressive toward humans and could live in peace with them became the ones who survived and reproduced. Thus, they created subsequent generations of cats who were progressively better adapted to living in harmony with people.

The ultimate result of this selection pressure over millennia is the modern cat, *Felis catus*. No matter if you own a tabby, Siamese, or Maine coon, they are all the same species. Individual breeds came much later, as cats were bred for specific traits. It is worth noting that cats are more biologically similar to their wild ancestors than dogs are to their wolf ancestors. The similarities between wild and domestic cats are important because they govern what an ideal, longevity-promoting diet looks like.

There are three factors to consider when choosing the best nutrition for your cat:

1. What nutrients are in the food?
2. How are the ingredients processed?
3. How much food is optimal?

(If you are fascinated by this topic and want to learn more details about feline nutrition, as well as the triumphs and failures of the modern pet-food industry, I would refer you to my first book, *The Ultimate Pet Health Guide*.)

1. WHAT NUTRIENTS ARE IN THE FOOD?

There are three sources of dietary energy (calories) in food: *protein*, *fat*, and *carbohydrates*. Literally, that is it; you can't get calories from anything else. Sometimes referred to as *macronutrients*, proteins, fats, and carbohydrates (along with water) provide your cat's body with the raw materials it needs to perform its necessary functions, like building muscle tissue, repairing a broken bone, or maintaining a normal immune system. In addition, micronutrients such as minerals and vitamins are also nutritionally necessary to promote health and longevity. Along with macronutrients, minerals such as calcium, magnesium, and zinc help make up the structure of tissues, while vitamins such as A, B, and C are needed to facilitate normal cellular functions and metabolism within the body.

The big difference between a biological system like your furry friend and an inanimate machine is that biology has an innate healing ability and tendency toward health.

In other words, your cat's body wants to be healthy, and given half a chance, it will stay that way. Conversely, if my car is broken, it is going to stay broken until someone (certainly not me!) fixes it. Even if I buy the needed parts for repair and put them next to the car, nothing is going to happen. In a biological system, on the other hand, often all that is needed is the raw materials and frequently the body will take it from there. But for our cats, we want more than just survival.

When there is a scarcity of one or more nutrients, vitamins, or minerals, the body has to make tough decisions—it has to triage. If you have ever been to a busy human or veterinary emergency room, you have likely experienced triage, with the medical staff prioritizing who is in the most need of care. It turns out a biological system is capable of internal triage.

Have you ever seen a malnourished cat? Of course the cat was shockingly underweight, but there is more to it than that. What did their hair coat look like? What was their energy level and demeanor? When faced with inadequate nutrients, the body has to prioritize, and first on the list is maintaining function of vital organs and the central nervous system. Everything else, like muscle mass, skin and coat, reproductive function, and energy to interact with the environment, takes a back seat. If you have spent time working at a shelter or watch rescue videos online, you have also seen what that cat looks like a few months after being rescued. Suddenly they have better muscle mass and are more interactive. They may even be unrecognizable because their coat is now full and healthy.

Basically, when there is scarcity, the body must plan for today. The prioritization list for micro- and macronutrients is lengthy, and for the body, limiting aging is going to be way, way down on the list; longevity is a future problem.[2]

This is the context within which to think about nutrition for longevity. We need to provide the body with enough nutrients not only to maintain critical body function and a normal life span but also to eliminate the need for triage and to ward off the hallmarks of aging.

Protein

When it comes to protein for cats, really the only choice is animal proteins. Cats are carnivores, period. While it is possible to feed a dog a plant-based diet, cats are having none of it. While everything your cat eats doesn't have to be animal based, the large majority of their food, and certainly their protein, should be. Meat sources can potentially be from just about any animal, although I normally recommend sticking with mammals and birds. In a perfect world, fish would be an excellent protein source, but the oceans are not as clean as we would like them to be, and many fish contain toxins such as mercury and arsenic.[3] The greatest benefit from fish is the fats such as EPA and DHA, which can be supplemented safely by other means—more on this in Chapter 6.

Protein from animal sources can come from muscle meat or organs such as heart, liver, and kidneys. In the United States and other Western cultures, we don't eat a lot of organ meat, but much of the prized nutrition from animals comes from organs, which contain vitamins, minerals, and specific amino acids that may not be found in high quantities in muscle. This is especially true for cats, as they require the amino acid taurine, which is found in high concentrations in heart tissue. Most animal predators in the wild eat the organs of their prey first, instinctively knowing where the best nutrition is.

Proteins to sidestep are meat meal and meat by-products. These ingredients are used as a low-cost way to increase the protein content of both kibble and canned diets. They are produced from the leftovers of meat production, and you have no way of knowing what is actually in them, leaving the quality and nutrient content of the protein a complete mystery. Feeding your cat is about transparency, knowing exactly what fuel you are putting in them. Clearly, meat meal and by-products do not make the cut. The good news is, meal and by-products are easily avoided, as they are listed as such on the ingredients label.

We can't get around the fact that there are some indirect problems to address when considering meat-based proteins. Meat production has a huge environmental impact in terms of greenhouse gases and water and land use.[4] A study from 2017 reported that annual dog- and cat-food consumption was responsible for 64 million tons of greenhouse gases.[5] That's a hard number to ignore. While meat is certainly the most evolutionarily and biologically appropriate food source for our pets, clearly it comes at a cost, and ultimately, environmental impacts are a longevity issue for all of us.

There is a promising solution on the horizon that allows our pets to "have their meat and eat it too": cultured proteins. Cultured protein is meat that doesn't come from an animal—sort of. The meat is produced from animal cells that are grown, or cultured, to produce meat. There is not an actual cow, pig, or chicken involved in the process, only the cells from one. It sounds a little freaky, but once perfected, cultured meat will have all the nutritional value of traditional meat without the environmental footprint or the need for millions of animals to be farmed. The ecological impact alone will be enormous.

For the time being, cultured meat is still in development. For humans, cultured protein will have to be not only nutritionally correct but also aesthetically pleasing. In other words, it's going to have to look like a T-bone or no one will buy it. Our cats, however, aren't too hung up on what their food looks like, and pets will be the first big benefactors of environmentally conscious meat protein.

Fats

Fats have multiple roles in your cat's body. They act as a source of stored energy; make up a large part of the skin, cell membranes, and nervous tissue; play a vital role in the absorption of other nutrients; and are involved in a wide array of metabolic processes. Your cat needs dietary fats to survive, thrive, and ensure a long and happy life.

Dietary fats can come from a variety of animal and plant sources, although for cats, as dedicated carnivores, the fat that accompanies the animal protein often makes up the majority of what they need. Plant-based fats can still be nutritionally beneficial and can be used in cat foods. When I designed recipes for cats in *The Ultimate Pet Health Guide,* plant-based oils were part of them. Additionally, there are specific longevity benefits to some plant-based fat supplements, as you will read in Chapter 6.

Naturally, when people think about nutrition for their cat, they tend to transfer what they know (or think they know) about human nutrition and then apply it to their choices of cat food. While the ideal nutrient profile for a person is somewhat different from a cat's, a lot of the assumptions people might make about ideal nutrition carry over. When it comes to dietary fats, however, there are two important differences between us and our cats.

As humans, we are frequently concerned about cholesterol. Diets high in cholesterol can lead to fatty deposits building up in our arteries, which over time can lead to a sudden loss of blood supply to the heart muscle (heart attack) or part of the brain (stroke). This is the reason why people are encouraged to avoid a lot of saturated fats that come from meat in favor of unsaturated fats from plant oils. The great news about your cat is that they don't build up cholesterol in their blood vessels and almost never have heart attacks or strokes. So, your cat can eat saturated fats from meats and not have any ill effects.

The other big difference in fat metabolism between cats and humans is that of omega-3 fatty acids. Omega-3s are often called essential fatty acids (EFAs) because the body cannot make them and therefore they must come from dietary sources. The most important EFAs are eicosapentaenoic acid (EPA) and docosahexaenoic acid (DHA), which are derived from marine sources such as fish, krill, plankton, and algae. EPA and DHA play vital roles in the body, including nervous system function, eye health, gut health, cardiovascular health, and more. This is why measuring omega fatty acid levels, as discussed in Chapter 2, is so critical to longevity. As humans, we can consume another omega-3, alpha-linolenic acid (ALA), from plant sources such as flax oil or hempseed oil and our bodies will convert the ALA to EPA and, to a lesser extent, DHA. Cats are largely unable to do this, so their EPA and DHA must originate from marine sources. This is why so many cats are deficient in omega-3 fatty acids.

But what about toxins? Because supplemental oils like fish oil are a purified product, they can be easily tested by third-party labs for contaminants such as heavy metals and other environmental toxins. Realize, however, that for all supplements there is no legal requirement for products to be tested or the results of the tests to be made public, so in Chapter 6 we'll discuss what to look for in good-quality supplements.

Carbohydrates

Sugars, starches, and cellulose, all of which originate from plants, make up what we call carbohydrates. While cats don't need carbohydrates, some amount in the diet can provide the body with an energy source (sugar) and, in the case of indigestible carbohydrates, fiber that aids in digestion.

The carbohydrate question for cats directly relates to the previous topic of an ancestral diet. As you know, cats are carnivores, full stop. A colleague of mine once said, "You will never see a lion drag home an ear of corn." It's a comical visual and also very true. Cats in the wild, including feral domestic cats, are hunters. Sure, they may be spotted nibbling on a little grass here and there, but at the end of the day, they are filling their bellies with other animals. And animals don't contain carbohydrates.

For makers of kibble, carbohydrates are a filler and a source of calories that are cheaper than meat. Kibble is basically a baked good, and the common ingredient found in all baked goods—whether we are talking about bread, cake, or kibble—is carbohydrates. You can't make baked goods without a carbohydrate source. Carb sources include grains, legumes (beans), potatoes, and so forth. So, when pet-food companies make the dough that ultimately becomes kibble, they use high levels of carbohydrates to increase nutrient density and ensure the kibble holds together.

Our cats' ancestors consumed minimal amounts of carbohydrates in their diet—let's say less than 5 percent. That "baked good" dry cat food is usually between 45 and 75 percent. Canned food is significantly less, although like kibble it is highly processed—which we will discuss later—and not optimal nutrition. The thing is, biology is forgiving, and even our carnivorous cats are able to find a way to utilize carbohydrates in their diet. Many cats, being the creatures of routine they are, become so acclimated to kibble, they are functionally "dry food addicted" and will only eat these foods. That said, if you put real meat and high-carb kibble in front of a domestic cat that is acclimated to eating a fresh-food diet, which one do you think they are going to eat?

While it is true that high-carbohydrate foods will support your cat's basic needs, these diets are not the optimal fuel for their biological function. High carbs can lead to weight gain, inflammatory conditions such as arthritis, and ultimately a shortened life span. Unlike dogs, whose evolutionary diet contains more carbohydrates, cats don't really "want" them in any significant quantity. As it pertains to the discussion about longevity, cats and large amounts of carbs really don't mix.

Water

Clearly, water is an important part of the diet for all living beings. When cats consume water, they get it from their water bowl or their food. On some level, it doesn't matter that much which bowl it comes from, although cats are frequently not the best water drinkers. In the wild, cats get most of their water from the prey they consume and don't stop to drink water all that often. In addition, cats can be finicky about their water bowl. They tend to prefer fresh, moving water, which is why they frequently like drinking from the faucet or even your water glass. If their water bowl is too small and their whiskers touch the sides, they may not want to use it. If the water is not fresh, they may not want to drink it. One good solution to encourage water drinking is a recirculating water bowl. These bowls have carbon filters to keep the water fresh, and the movement frequently leads cats to investigate and take a drink.

Given their peculiarities around drinking water, it is better for kitties if the water they consume comes from their food. Maintaining adequate hydration is critical to optimizing function of every system in the body. Even mild dehydration can put stress on the kidneys, blood flow, tissue oxygenation, nutrient absorption, and so forth. Every one of the 14 hallmarks of aging is negatively impacted by dehydration.

When a cat is eating a fresh-food diet (more on this in the "Frozen, Freeze-Dried, and Fresh" section on page 70), they are getting a lot of water with every bite they take. Water is necessary in order for food to be properly broken down, as well as aiding digestion and nutrient absorption, so having the water come along with the food is better all around. It may be that the water bowl is right next to your cat's food bowl, but you can't make them drink out of it for all the reasons just discussed. Something I hear from pet owners all the time after they switch their cat to a high-water-content diet like fresh food is that their cat barely, if ever, drinks out of the water bowl anymore. Another little hack is to add a bit of water to the food bowl to further increase water consumption. Bottom line: the more water your kitty is getting in their food, the better.

There is also the question of water quality. Depending on where you live, your tap water may or may not be clean. We are all familiar with some of the life-threatening water-quality issues that have occurred in places like Flint, Michigan. What you may not be aware of is that tap water in many areas has been shown to be contaminated with pharmaceuticals, agricultural chemicals, and other toxins.[6]

Unless you live someplace where the water quality is exceptionally good, you might consider a water-purification system like reverse osmosis because—sorry to say it—those countertop pitchers that filter water really just don't make the grade.

Reverse osmosis costs a little money, but this particular upgrade is really as much for the humans in the house as it is for the cats. It is important for the reverse-osmosis system to have a remineralization feature to replace minerals that are removed during the purification process. Without this, over the long term, reverse-osmosis water can cause a loss of minerals in the body. I've had a reverse-osmosis water purifier under my kitchen sink for years, so all our water for drinking, cooking, and ice is filtered. After you have been drinking properly filtered water for a little while, you become very aware when you drink water that isn't. You can literally taste the difference. I don't know how to describe poor water quality other than that it tastes like chemicals, and it always makes me grateful that I get to go home and drink clean water. As an alternative to reverse osmosis, you could consider bottled water or a water-delivery service, but that can get expensive or be cumbersome. Ultimately, do what works best for you.

Vitamins and Minerals

Vitamins A, B, C, D, E, and K are organic compounds that must be present in the diet in order for normal body functions to be maintained. For example, vitamin A is needed to maintain normal vision, immune system function, and reproductive ability. In the previous chapter, we discussed how most cats have deficient vitamin D levels and how that impacts the hallmarks of aging. Thinking again of internal triage, if a cat is facing a deficiency, such as a lack of vitamin

D, their body has to decide where to allocate what little it has. Vitamin D is a critical part of calcium absorption, and it also reduces inflammation and helps protect the body from cancer. If we consider the body of the severely malnourished cat from before, it will use vitamin D to maintain the biological processes most necessary for life, such as proper immune system function. If vitamin D is deficient to the point where the body can't properly absorb and maintain adequate calcium in the bones, they will lose their strength and rigidity. To be clear, there aren't too many cats out there who are so deficient in vitamin D that they have the "soft" bones associated with the clinical disease known as rickets. That doesn't mean they aren't deficient at all and might not still be suffering some ill effects such as poor immunity and a greater risk of cancer.

In addition to vitamins, minerals are inorganic compounds such as calcium, potassium, iron, and sodium. Along with protein, fat, carbs, and water, minerals are used to create and maintain every tissue in the body. Mineral deficiencies can lead to all manner of diseases. A lack of potassium, for example, will lead to a loss of muscle strength and coordination and, in severe cases, disturbances of heart rhythm. Magnesium, as we have previously discussed, is associated with accelerated aging and is another frequent deficiency for cats. In short, vitamins and minerals are critical to maintain the basic functions of life on a day-to-day basis and promote both life span and health span.

2. HOW ARE THE INGREDIENTS PROCESSED?

When it comes to longevity-focused nutrition, having the proper micro- and macronutrients is critical. But have you considered how those nutrients are prepared and presented to your cat? The basis of food preparation that focuses on health and longevity has everything to do with preserving the nutrition that Mother Nature put in there. In the last section we talked about the importance of proteins, fats, carbs, water, vitamins, and minerals individually, but in reality, that is not how nutrition works. Food sources are not exclusively protein, fat, or vitamins. Animal products, for example, are a combination of protein, fat, vitamins, minerals, and water. Lots of ingredients in one package.

Here is an indisputable fact: every animal species on the planet evolved eating a fresh, whole-foods diet. All their nutrition came from the whole foods they ate. Remember the metaphor of the car and how it is designed to function optimally with specific types of fuel and fluids? When it comes to animals—you and your cat included—we are designed to receive all our micro- and macronutrients through whole foods. The concept of food processing, preservation, and supplements is a human construct designed to provide convenience. There are still benefits associated with appropriate supplementation (see Chapter 6), but in a perfect world, all these vitamins and minerals would be introduced into the body through the whole foods eaten.

Kibble and Canned Foods

You don't need a Ph.D. in nutrition to know that eating more fresh, whole foods and fewer processed foods is healthier. There certainly can be, and are, arguments about ideal diets such as keto, paleo, or vegan, but even at the fringes, no one is advocating for people to improve their health by eating large amounts of processed foods.

In 2020, over $40 billion was spent on pet food in the United States.[7] Of that $40 billion, the sales of fresh-food diets make up only 4 percent.[8] That means that 96 percent of the pet food sold in the United States is kibble and canned. Here's the thing, kibble and canned food primarily exist for one simple reason (and—surprise—it's the same reason processed foods are so prevalent in our diets): our convenience. Kibble and canned diets provide pet owners with a relatively inexpensive food option that won't spoil and has no need for refrigeration. Let me be very clear: no matter what the pet-food companies tell you, highly processed foods like kibble and canned food are not ideal nutrition.

There are two big problems with processed cat foods. For starters, they are manufactured at very high temperatures and, in the case of kibble, high pressure. The reason for this is simple: High-temperature and high-pressure processing is necessary if you are going to take fresh ingredients and make them shelf-stable. If you've accidentally overcooked vegetables so long that they turned into grayish-brown mush, beyond being unappetizing, a lot of the nutrition that was originally in those beautiful green veggies has been lost. It is the same with processed cat foods.

Most frequently what is lost are vitamins and other functional compounds such as enzymes. Pet-food companies often add vitamins back to the food after the processing, but the problem is that what is added back may not be as beneficial as what was lost. Naturally occurring vitamins are not so much a single molecule but a complex of phytonutrients. When we supplement a vitamin such as vitamin C, we are adding ascorbic acid, which is a portion of the vitamin C complex rather than the whole thing. As such, supplemented vitamins don't always work as well as those found naturally in whole foods. Additionally, the loss of enzymes or other bioactive compounds is generally not accounted for at all.

The other main issue is what is gained during processing. Specifically, the high temperature and pressure lead to chemical changes in food that have the potential to cause great harm to your cat. Maillard reaction products (MRPs) and advanced glycation end products (AGEs) are formed during the cooking process. In fact, the browning that occurs with cooking is a result of MRP formation. Research has shown MRPs and AGEs contribute to oxidative stress, which causes inflammation, organ disease, and even cancer, affecting most of the hallmarks of aging.[9 10]

Consumption of MRPs and AGEs in small amounts is probably fine (although less is better) for both humans and cats. Here's the rub: When researchers evaluated the amount of MRPs in processed pet foods, they found cats consume 122 times more per day than the average human. The data for AGEs revealed a daily intake 38 times higher than humans.[11] There is no other way to put it—this is not okay.

Frozen, Freeze-Dried, and Fresh

In the grand scheme of things, the best foods to feed your cat for longevity are balanced, fresh, whole foods. There are a few options to try. These days, in pet stores and online you can buy prepared frozen meals that are lightly cooked or raw. Freeze-dried raw diets are great too because the freeze-drying process occurs at low temperature and pressure, so we don't have the nutrient loss and MRP/AGE issue to worry about. These options also have the benefit of a very high water content, assuming you are adding water to the freeze-dried food as directed. Alternatively, you can make food at home. The caveat for home-prepared meals is that it's essential to work from a balanced recipe created by a nutritionist, such as the ones in *The Ultimate Pet Health Guide*. You cannot just put meat and veggies into a bowl and assume your cat is getting everything they need if you want them to live their best and longest life.

3. HOW MUCH FOOD IS OPTIMAL?

After learning that fresh, whole-food diets are a great way to support longevity, a lot of the cat owners I see in my practice are interested in how to implement them. Beyond the inquiries about specific brand or recipe recommendations, the most common question I am asked is "How much do I feed?"

Consider Calorie Restriction

Research in multiple species indicates that the number of calories consumed per day has a direct impact on longevity.[12] Specifically (although no one really wants to hear this), calorie restriction leads to an increased life span. There are a couple of reasons for this. The first is that calorie restriction upregulates (turns on) metabolic processes like autophagy that have a direct positive impact on the hallmarks of aging. Conversely, higher calorie intake leads to increased body fat, which is associated with inflammation and insulin resistance, both of which promote disease and aging.[13] So, your cat should be eating enough calories to maintain optimal body function and nothing extra.

Both the health and the longevity benefits of calorie restriction are about how often your cat eats as much as their daily caloric intake. It turns out that many of the hallmarks of aging are positively affected during periods of not eating, or what is known as intermittent fasting.[14] In dogs, for example, the current research indicates those who eat once daily have "better cognitive function and lower odds of having gastrointestinal, dental, orthopedic, kidney/urinary, and liver/pancreas disorders" compared to those eating more than once daily.[15] Similarly, there is research to support benefits for cats as well.[16] To be clear, your cat would need the same amount of food as if they were eating twice daily, just fed in one meal rather than two. The time of day for the single meal is not super critical, and the best plan is to figure out what works for you and your kitty. Lastly, the benefits of once-daily eating require your cat to fast between those meals. That means few, if any, treats.

Calculate a Starting Point

I know you're thinking, *This is all very interesting, but* how much *should I feed my cat?* Your starting point should be based on the recommendation for the food you are using. If it is store-bought, the package will have some guidelines. If you are preparing the food, make sure the recipe offers how many calories there are per cup of food. Then you can calculate your cat's daily calorie requirement. The charts on this page and the next will help you determine your cat's resting energy requirement (RER) and daily energy requirement (DER). Ultimately, DER is the number of calories per day to feed, at least to begin with.

Body Weight (pounds)	Body Weight (kilograms)	RER in kcal/day
2	0.91	65
4	1.82	110
6	2.73	149
8	3.64	184
10	4.55	218
15	6.82	295
20	9.09	366
25	11.36	433

Activity	Cat DER
Weight loss	1.0 x RER
Neutered adult (normal activity)	1.2 x RER
Intact adult	1.4 x RER
Light activity	N/A
Moderate activity	1.6 x RER
Heavy activity	N/A
Pregnancy (0-42 days)	1.6 x RER (free feed)
Pregnancy (42 + days)	2 x RER (free feed)
Lactation	2.6 x RER (free feed)
Kitten (weaning to 4 months)	2.5 x RER
Kitten (4 months to adult size)	2.5 x RER

You should also consider your cat's body condition score (BCS). As shown in the chart on page 74, BCS is evaluated on a 9-point scale, with 5 being ideal. Below 5 is underweight, and above 5 is overweight. Given what we know about calorie restriction and longevity, I recommend shooting for a BCS of between 4.5 and 5. Regardless of whether you are determining the amount to feed from the recommendations on the package or are calculating DER, it is important to aim for your cat's optimal body weight. In other words, if your cat weighs 15 pounds and has a BCS of 6, their optimal body weight is probably closer to 12 or 13 pounds, or maybe a little less. Calculate the amount to feed based on the weight they *should* be.

1	Can't feel any fat when touching cat's body. Ribs clearly observable by sight alone on short-haired cats. Upper hip bone and lower vertebrae (lumbar) easily felt by hand. Extreme abdominal tuck.
2	Can't feel any fat when touching cat's body. Ribs clearly observable by sight on short-haired cats. Lumbar vertebrae are easily felt and contain only a slight bit of muscle around them. Prominent abdominal tuck.
3	Small amounts of fat can be felt when touching cat's stomach. Ribs easily felt by touch with only a slight layer of fat. Waist prominently tapers and stands out below ribs. Lumbar vertebrae are easily felt.
4	Lack of distinct and palpable fat pad. Ribs can be felt by touch under a slight layer of fat. Waist visibly tapers and stands out below ribs. Moderate abdominal tuck visible.
5	Slight palpable abdominal fat pad. Ribs can be felt under a small layer of fat. Visible waist below ribs, but without a sharp taper into body.
6	Ribs can be felt under a minimal amount of extra fat. No visible abdominal tuck. Abdominal fat layer and waist are both discernible but not prominent.
7	Waist is difficult to see. Ribs have noticeable fat covering and are not easily felt. Noticeable abdominal fat pad. Stomach is beginning to become bulbous.
8	No discernible waist. Ribs cannot be felt due to large amount of fat. Fat pockets developing around lower back (lumbar vertebrae). Stomach is clearly bulbous and has pronounced fat pad.
9	No waist whatsoever, with a stomach that is bulbous and hangs beneath the body. Many abdominal fat pockets as well as excess fat around the limbs, face, and lumbar spine area. Ribs cannot be felt, covered with significant layer of fat.

Any formulas or charts are able to provide you with only a starting point, because regardless of how it is calculated, the recommended daily amount to feed your cat is a guess that hinges on both internal (metabolism) and external (exercise) factors. A friend who is a veterinary internal-medicine specialist once told me that calculating daily calorie requirements for cats is only something interns do. Here is my "highly scientific" advice: After you calculate a starting point for feeding, keep an eye on your cat's weight and BCS. If they are getting fat, feed them less. If they are getting skinny, feed them more. At the end of the day, it's as simple as that.

PRACTICAL CONSIDERATIONS

Feeding your cat for longevity requires consideration of food ingredients, preparation, amount, and frequency. There is no question that a properly balanced, fresh, whole-food diet fed in the right amount gives your cat the best nutritional advantage for a long and healthy life, and in a vacuum, the chapter ends here. In the real world, however, there are other factors to consider. The biggest challenges pet owners face when it comes to nutrition for their cat (or themselves) are the age-old issues of time and money.

Fresh-food diets necessarily require a commitment of either time or money, although frequently both are involved. Fresh food, regardless of whether it is for humans or cats, is always going to be more expensive than processed foods. This is why nutrition-related illnesses are so common in people who are economically disadvantaged. Calories from processed foods are cheaper and easier to obtain.

If you own one cat, the price of premade fresh food may be within reach. If you own multiple cats, you could easily find yourself spending hundreds of dollars per month on frozen cooked or raw foods. Let's be honest, for most of us, that is going to be tough to sustain. On the flip side, if you make food at home, there is a time commitment, but you can purchase the individual ingredients yourself and the costs per meal will be significantly lower. In addition, you have control over sourcing ingredients, such as finding a good butcher who can save cuts of meat that are great for cats but maybe don't sell well for humans. Trimmings from high-quality cuts of meat can be both affordable and nutritious. If organic is within the budget, I highly encourage it. That said, I will choose a conventional fresh-food diet over organic kibble any day.

The bottom line is, whatever you do regarding feeding your cat, you have to go with a plan that is sustainable for your life. If you love spending time in the kitchen, it may be that making food is for you. If you don't even know how to turn on your stove, perhaps not. You can also make as much food as you are able in one go and then portion and freeze. If you can make a couple of weeks' (or more) worth of food all at once, this cuts down your time in the kitchen drastically. There is certainly no need to be doing food prep multiple times per week.

Or you might consider feeding a combination of store-bought fresh food and homemade. And if feeding all fresh food is too much of a financial challenge, feed as much as you can afford and supplement the rest with high-quality canned food or kibble. Read ingredients lists to make sure they contain real meat (not meat meal or by-products). For dry foods, make sure that they are relatively low in carbohydrates. There are also some air-dried kibbles out there that are better than the more conventionally produced kibble. If it is air-dried, you will see it prominently listed on the packaging, as this is a selling point for the company. At the end of the day, we all have to live in the real world, and reconsidering what you feed your cat isn't an all-or-nothing proposition.

One final note regarding diets: variety is a plus. Cats evolved to eat a spectrum of foods that contain an array of proteins, fats, and other nutrients. Feeding them the same ingredients for years may have detrimental effects, such as the development of food sensitivities. Instead, I highly recommend rotating through different recipes over time. Depending on how sensitive your cat is to dietary changes, you can do this as often as daily or as infrequently as several times per year. If your cat is sensitive to food changes, make sure to gradually transition from one diet to the next over a week or so.

* * *

While nutrition is unquestionably "step one" when it comes to longevity, exercise and lifestyle come in a close second. In the next chapter, we will discover how to build on our foundation of nutrition by exploring ways to create a longevity-promoting environment at home for your furry friends.

CHAPTER 4

EXERCISE AND LIFESTYLE

While optimizing your cat's diet is the foundation for their longevity, providing them with an appropriate amount of exercise and promoting a healthy lifestyle are right up there in terms of importance. The great news about exercise and lifestyle adjustments, compared to just about everything else we discuss in this book, is that they are totally free. Everyone can implement these changes regardless of finances, and when done correctly, you will have a huge positive impact on your cat's quality of life and longevity, not to mention your own.

In this chapter we'll explore the positive effects of exercise and how to make sure your cat is getting enough movement daily. I'll give you some ideas for how to incorporate play into your indoor cat's routine, as well as how to maintain activity in an arthritic cat. A major part of a healthy lifestyle for a cat involves reducing any anxiety, so I'll outline some of the common sources of stress and how to alleviate them.

EXERCISE

For humans, science has been wishy-washy when it comes to what exercise works best for health and longevity. Theories and recommendations come and go. Aerobic exercise was the primary goal for a while. Later those recommendations were replaced with a greater focus on resistance training. Then it was cross-training, then high-intensity interval training—the beat goes on. Through the years, the experts have debated what kind of, and how much, exercise is best for us humans, but the constant they all agree on is that moving our bodies is essential to maintain good health. It's an undeniable fact that an appropriate amount of exercise makes a body stronger and healthier.

Not surprisingly, this is all as true for cats as it is for humans. We know a lack of exercise can lead to weight gain (in fat), muscle loss, joint pain, and, in many cases, poor health. While much of the information in this book can be applied to both cats and dogs, when it comes to exercise, these animals are quite different. After all, not too many of us are taking our cats out for leash walks and playing fetch at the park. That said, exercise is just as important for cats as it is for dogs and people.

As we move into this chapter about exercise and lifestyle, we begin by answering one very important question: Indoor or outdoor?

From a medical perspective, there really is no need for debate. While it is true that cats going outside tend to get more exercise and maintain a better body weight, the price is way, way too high. According to the veterinary school at University of California–Davis, indoor cats have an average life span of 10 to 15 years, while outdoor cats average 2 to 5 years.[1] The reasons for this are pretty apparent. An outdoor environment is fraught with dangers, including cars, attacks from other animals (wild and domestic), injuries, toxins, and so forth.

If you're still not convinced you need to keep your cat indoors, consider this: Remember in the last chapter when we discussed that cats are carnivores? Well, when your kitty is outside, they are on the hunt, and the results are devastating to the ecosystem. Studies suggest domestic cats are responsible for killing as many as 22.3 billion mammals and 4 billion birds in the United States annually.[2] If you are a cat lover, then hopefully you are, more broadly speaking, an animal lover too. Outdoor cats are a danger to themselves and much of the wildlife in your neighborhood. There is no way to say it other than this is not okay.

The good news is that if cats never go outside, they generally don't want to go outside. If you keep your cat indoors from day one, having a strictly indoor cat is easy. Don't be fooled by the sentiment that they are missing out on something by being kept indoors. If that pulls at your heartstrings, please reread the two previous paragraphs. If you really, really want your cat to have some outdoor time, there are some pretty cool easy-to-set-up outdoor enclosures for cats that allow them to see, hear, and smell the outside without exposing them to outdoor hazards or placing the local wild critters in danger.

Admittedly, it can be challenging to convert an outdoor cat to indoor status. Sometimes they can be slowly acclimated, and outdoor enclosures may allow them the feeling of being outside and keep them happy. There are, however, going to be cats that refuse to become indoor cats. Honestly, I really don't have a solution beyond planning to make all your future feline charges strictly indoor residents.

Effects of Exercise

Cats are natural athletes, and acrobatics are part of their built-in repertoire, so exercise-related injuries are uncommon. When they don't get to utilize those abilities, however, they can get restless and potentially destructive. The challenge with keeping cats strictly indoors is that we, as their caretakers, need to provide them with an environment that keeps them healthy and stimulated. Inadequate physical stimulation in cats can lead to decreased mobility as they age (due to decreased muscle mass), bad behaviors associated with stress and anxiety, and even cognitive decline. Many, if not all, of these factors relate back to the hallmarks of aging, and regular exercise is one of the tools we have to address and improve bodily processes that lead to a cat being physically old, regardless of their chronological age.

The effects of exercise on the body can be evaluated on multiple levels, starting with whole-body macro function, as well as drilling down all the way to cellular and subcellular effects, as described in Chapter 1. Beginning with macro effects, cats who get regular exercise maintain lean body mass and have better muscle strength, cardiovascular health, stamina, balance, and mobility. Obesity in cats can lead to increased incidence of diabetes, joint pain, hypertension, and cancer. Interestingly, one study evaluating longevity in cats revealed that slightly overweight cats actually lived longer than cats that weighed less.[3] To be clear, obesity is a health risk, but it may be that a little extra padding provides some protection from disease conditions that lead to weight loss, such as chronic kidney failure.

One other big-picture piece that may not be as obvious is how exercise affects the cognitive function of older cats. Exercise's physical and psychological benefits are proven in the oldest humans, as higher exercise capacity is noted as a significant factor in the longevity of people over 100 years old.[4] There is every reason to believe this is the case for our cats as well. In fact, studies on both animals and humans confirm that regular physical exercise is associated with better cognitive function in geriatric individuals.[5] Declines in cognition are a serious problem in geriatric cats and frequently manifest as decreased interaction with their owners and behaviors like crying out or restlessness and anxiety, particularly at night. Quality of life for both cat and owner becomes a major issue when people aren't sleeping because their cat is vocalizing throughout the night. In short, exercise equals happier cats who live longer and have better mental acuity.

Moving deeper into the cellular effects of exercise, research indicates that it has a positive impact on literally every single one of the original nine hallmarks of aging.[6] That's right, all of them. So, yes, exercise will help your cat have more stamina and stay lean and will likely improve their mental state, but the bigger gains occur on a much less visible level. As we continue to shine a light on the various interventions we can undertake to help our cats live longer and healthier lives, you will find that diet and exercise are the only two to have such a broad impact. Though previously I described optimizing nutrition as the foundation of health and longevity, the truth is that achieving a significant extension of your cat's life span and health span—their quantity and quality of life—requires optimizing nutrition *as well as* exercise and lifestyle.

Getting Physical

So how do you exercise your kitty? It will come as no surprise to any cat owner that exercise requirements vary from cat to cat. When considering optimal exercise, we need to evaluate who your cat is from the perspective of their age, personal tendencies, and energy levels.

You already know the reasons why cats should stay indoors, and for the purposes of this discussion, we will focus on indoor cats. Outdoor cats are pretty much going to do their own thing, for better or for worse, and much of what they do is out of our control. Exercise and activity for indoor cats, however, is within our control, and it is critical to both their physical and mental health—possibly in ways you might not even realize.

It is true that indoor cats tend to get less exercise than ones that spend time outdoors. With indoor cats, we also have to be more cognizant of their weight, as the tendency is toward heaviness. Some of this can be managed through diet—high-carbohydrate foods like kibble are much more likely to pack on the pounds than an appropriate fresh-food diet. Engaging kitties in play is also an important way to manage both their weight and their overall physical fitness.

Now, if you have more than one cat, it may be that they keep each other fit by chasing one another around the house in those short bursts of energy that all cats have. For single-cat households, however, kitties can get pretty lazy and lounge about most of the day, leading to fat gain and muscle loss.

A good rule of thumb is to engage your cat in play at least a couple of times per day for between 10 and 30 minutes, depending on their attention span. Getting cats to exercise is all about appealing to their predatory instincts. They like to hunt and chase. You can get them going by throwing toys they can pounce on or using a stick with feathers at the end of a string. There are also toys that drop treats when your cat plays with them; a reward for exercising can be a great way to get your cat moving. Laser pointers can also be a fun toy to use with cats, although I recommend giving your kitty a reward, such as a treat, after a few minutes, because it can be frustrating for them to chase after that red dot and never be able to catch it.

The key to success is figuring out what is stimulating to your kitty; anything that your cat gets excited about will help support a healthy body weight. Sometimes a paper grocery bag or a cardboard box is all it takes to get them going.

Maintaining Activity in an Arthritic Cat

In the discussion of diagnostic testing in Chapter 2, I mentioned a lab called VDI that looks at a variety of factors associated with aging and injury that are not generally found on the standard blood panel your veterinarian might run. A couple of them can be helpful in both diagnosis of joint injuries and arthritis and monitoring of treatment efficacy—specifically, serum hyaluronic acid (sHA) and haptoglobin (HPT).

Hyaluronic acid (HA) is the viscous liquid within the joints that provides lubrication. When there is inflammation in one or more joints due to injury or arthritis, HA can leak into the bloodstream. So, sHA is a marker that can be used to measure the level of joint inflammation present in a cat. HPT is more of a measure of inflammation within the entire body. HPT can be elevated for a wide variety of reasons, including acute infection or inflammation in one or more body tissues, such as joints. A test that combines sHA levels with HPT can provide a window onto the level of joint inflammation your kitty is experiencing. This can be particularly useful information in cats whose activity level has decreased but it is not clear if this could be due to arthritis. You and your veterinarian can also use these diagnostic tests to measure the effectiveness of treatments to mitigate joint inflammation.*

As in arthritic people, it is critical to maintain a healthy level of activity for kitties with arthritis. Their natural tendency is to be less active, so it is important to continue to encourage them to move around. Inactivity leads to decreased muscle mass, which in turn leads to more unstable joints and more joint-related pain. That said, excessive activity, such as jumping or playing too much, can lead to joint inflammation and pain. The key with arthritic cats is to keep them moving around, even if it is just walking or playing for a few minutes several times daily to maintain or improve their level of function.

LIFESTYLE

When people think about their cat's lifestyle, they probably assume they are living like a king or a queen without a care in the world. Keep in mind, though, that a cat's disposition and worldview, just like their diet, is greatly affected by their evolutionary nature. As you know, cats are predators, and usually solitary ones. In the wild, they would constantly be on the lookout for their next meal and for potential dangers. While neither of these things is a "real" concern for your pampered kitty, their brain still works like that of a predator, and their environment at home can either promote feelings of fulfillment and security or leave them feeling unsettled or unsafe. Exercise; environmental enrichment; and interactions with other cats, nonfeline pets, and people can all have a profound effect on a cat's lifestyle and sense of well-being.

* There are many options, from Western medicine to holistic alternatives, to treat joint injury, inflammation, and arthritis in cats. For readers who are interested in a comprehensive deep dive into these options, you will find Chapter 12 of my first book, *The Ultimate Pet Health Guide*, to be filled with details and actionable information.

Stress and Anxiety

Let's talk about kitty stress and anxiety a little. A lot of people have asked me how their cat can possibly be stressed given that they have a perfect life, with all their needs met. The reality is, stress doesn't always have to do with hardship, and understanding the factors that can cause anxiety in cats is key to supporting a healthy lifestyle for your cat.

A lot of things can lead to anxiety in cats. Certainly, a lack of activity and exercise can be one of them. As we discussed, cats are predators, and given the opportunity, they are going to hunt. This is stimulating for them both physically and mentally. If they are not outside hunting, we can scratch that itch by letting them chase toys that rattle or squeak (simulating prey) or even by training them to hunt for treats.

Put Your Cat's Instincts to Work

One great way to get your cat moving is to appeal to their love of the hunt. Try this out by placing treats around the house in places where your cat normally goes, and then give them the satisfaction of finding them. When your kitty starts looking for the treats in the "usual" places, move them around a little. Make the moving of the treats gradual so it is easy for the cat to find them at first. Keep moving the treats around to different areas and sometimes back to previous areas. The goal here is for them to get in the habit of looking (hunting). Eventually, you can get creative with the hiding places, and they will start prowling the house in search of what has been left. This is a great way to tap into their predatory nature!

Having more than one cat in the house can be a great way for them to get physical and mental stimulation. It can also present problems, as there are times when cats don't get along. Usually, one is dominant, and the submissive one feels threatened. Sometimes this is obvious, because one cat chases or beats up on the other. Other times the interactions between the cats can be subtle. Cats don't have very expressive faces, at least from the perspective of us humans. That said, a dominant stare from one cat to another can really ratchet up the anxiety level of the recipient.

Another source of anxiety for cats is, well . . . just about anything. Cats are like little people with obsessive-compulsive disorder (OCD). They want everything to be the same every day, and if something changes, well then, clearly as their caregiver, you were asking for that tantrum! Problematic changes can come in the form of new animals or people in the house, animals or people normally in the house who are missing, moving to a new home, loud noises such as construction, or even rearranging the furniture. Certainly, cats are resilient, and most of them will not go into a tailspin if you get a new couch. Just understand that something that may be so subtle as to be unnoticeable to you could be a really big deal for your cat.

So how can you tell if your kitty is stressed or anxious? There are several common signs. Just like stressed-out humans, kitties can get cranky. They may be less affectionate or even outright angry. Also, note that cats are notorious for displacing their aggression. If they are angry about something, they will often lash out at whoever innocently crosses their path, be it another animal or a human. (I bet you have met a few people in your life who have the same tendency.)

Another way cats manifest anxiety is through overgrooming. Clearly, grooming is part of normal kitty behavior.

In addition to keeping their fur in order, grooming is a self-soothing behavior. The familiarity of it calms them down (coming back to that whole OCD thing again). But when they are stressed, they will frequently overgroom, which can result in loss of fur, usually on their belly or sides. A good way to differentiate this from hair loss due to allergies is that with anxiety, their skin frequently looks fine. No redness, scabs, and so forth. They will often also show "barbering" of the fur, meaning the fur is still there, but it is shorter because the hair shafts are broken from the grooming. This tells us the hair is not falling out but being groomed away.

The third manifestation of kitty displeasure is both the most common and the most problematic for a lot of people. Anxious or upset cats tend to urinate outside the litter box. This could be right next to the box or anywhere else in your house, including, unfortunately, your pillow. You have to admit—as a form of protest, it is definitely an attention-getter. Inappropriate urination in cats can actually have both emotional and physical underpinnings. Anxious or stressed cats may urinate outside the box purely to voice their displeasure with something. That said, anxious cats also tend to do, or actually *not* do, something else: they drink less water.

As previously mentioned, cats in the wild are not naturally big water drinkers, as they obtain a lot of their water from food. When they are stressed, they are even less likely to go to the water bowl. This is going to be much less of an issue for cats eating fresh-food diets, since they naturally have a high water content, but for cats eating kibble, this can cause a real problem.

When they aren't drinking enough and start to become dehydrated, their bodies retain water by concentrating their urine. As the urine gets more concentrated, minerals can crystallize and form something that looks like sand in their urinary bladder. The highly concentrated urine and crystals are extremely irritating to the bladder, leading to inflammation and discomfort. Essentially, they have the symptoms of a urinary tract infection without the infection. The result is they have an increased urgency to urinate, and they tend to do so whenever the urge hits, meaning frequently outside the box. This type of irritation is called either *feline urologic syndrome (FUS)* or *feline lower urinary tract disease (FLUTD)*. The terms are interchangeable.

For some male cats, the crystals can clump together near the tip of the penis and create an obstruction, preventing them from urinating. A urinary obstruction is 100 percent a life-threatening emergency and must be treated immediately. Note that this only happens in male cats, because their urethra is much narrower than females'. Both males and females can get FLUTD, but only a male can get obstructed. If you have a male cat that seems to be straining to urinate, take them to a veterinarian immediately, day or night.

How You Can Help

Mitigating long-term anxiety can be as challenging for cats as it is for humans. First things first: it's important to realize that you can improve things, but you can't necessarily fix them. I don't mean for this to sound discouraging, because a lot of gains can be made with highly stressed cats. And, regardless of how stress or anxiety manifests, it is a sign that some lifestyle changes may be needed, particularly if you are dealing with a recurring or ongoing issue.

There are three main focuses in alleviating the effects of long-term stress and anxiety:

1. **Secure living arrangement:** Create an indoor living environment that minimizes stress. This means understanding if your cat is stressed by other animals in the house and reducing that stress as much as possible.
2. **Routine:** The bedrock of helping cats with anxiety is providing consistency to their days. This includes a stable routine and regular play/exercise time.
3. **Supplements and medications:** Depending on the circumstances, natural supplements can be beneficial. One such product that has received a lot of attention is CBD. CBD for animals has gained widespread use and acceptance in recent years, and it has long been used to help alleviate stress and anxiety. While CBD is generally safe for cats, it is best to consult with a knowledgeable source when it comes to product selection and dosing. If your veterinarian is unable to assist, you can find valuable information through the Veterinary Cannabis Society (VCS.pet) and VeterinaryCannabis.org. In addition to natural supplementation, drugs like fluoxetine sometimes work in severe cases of anxiety, but only when used in conjunction with changes to the environment.

When considering a person with an anxiety disorder, such as a panic disorder, social anxiety, and so forth, you can't simply medicate the problem away. Meds may be helpful, but the real gains are made (1) by ensuring basic needs are met, and (2) through ongoing therapy. For your cat, therapy comes in the form of attention and positive interactions. This provides structure, which in turn gives your cat a sense of stability and certainty.

Cats thrive on schedules and knowing what to expect from their day. Think about the kinds of things you get stressed-out about—perhaps what your boss is going to say at your next review, how much your tax bill is going to be, or if you are going to find your soulmate. I'd be willing to wager that most or all of the things you are worrying about have roots in some kind of uncertainty. When you or your cat is not obsessing over the unknown, your stress levels are reduced dramatically.

Multiple-Animal Dynamics

We know that optimal nutrition for cats is based on the nutrient profile they evolved eating, and the same is true when it comes to lifestyle. Cats, with the exception of lions, live solitary lives outside of mating season. Certainly, when we look at colonies of feral cats, they do reside together. When they are free living outside, they are easily able to keep a comfortable distance from one another when it suits them. In a household environment, on the other hand, keeping a distance can become a problem.

There are plenty of strictly indoor multicat households where everyone gets along just fine. It is quite common, however, for there to be friction between cats. As discussed, cats can be a source of stress for one another in ways that are sometimes obvious, such as one cat attacking another, and sometimes subtle, such as a dominant stare from across the room.

The decision to add cat number two, three, or more to the household has to be made with careful consideration given to the personalities and dynamics of the cat(s) already in the house. Some cats are very social and easygoing, and adding a kitty is easy. In other cases, there can be challenges, and sometimes peaceful coexistence is impossible.

When introducing new cats into the house, here are a few things to consider:

- Getting a kitten or young adult will usually lead to less friction than adding an adult cat, as the young one will naturally be submissive to an older cat.
- If possible, get a cat that's the opposite sex of the one you already have. It's not written in stone, but on the whole, opposite sexes seem to get along better.
- Do a gradual introduction by placing the new cat in a room with the door closed. This will allow both cats to smell each other under the door and get used to their presence. After a couple of days, reverse the arrangement and allow the new cat to explore the main area a bit, while the older kitty is in the other room. Allow for this back-and-forth for at least one week.

Once the cats let you know the novelty of the other cat has worn off through their relative disinterest, you can introduce the cats by allowing them to see each other. If you can do this across a baby gate, that would be ideal. Be prepared for some hissing and general displeasure. Hopefully this won't last long, and you will be able to let them freely interact. They will have to establish their own dynamic, so there may be a few disagreements. As long as there is no outright fighting, allow them to sort it out. With any luck, they will be sleeping intertwined before you know it!

Usually these situations can be worked out, but there are circumstances where two cats just don't get along no matter what you do. (I've met a few people who fit that description.) In these cases, solutions may range from the cats living in separate areas of the house to supplements or medications for one or both cats to, as a last resort, rehoming one of the cats.

Of course, it's possible there are other animals at home beyond cats. Frequently, dogs and cats live in the same house. Most of the time, dogs and cats do well together. Often, the dog is curious about the cat, and when they get too close, the cat "corrects" them with a hiss and a swat. For most dogs, experiencing this once or twice is enough to learn the lesson. As is the case with two cats, it is best to introduce a dog and cat gradually and allow them to get used to one another's smell and presence before giving them free access to one another. Depending on their personalities, they might become fast friends or choose to peacefully coexist without much interaction.

The only time dog-and-cat cohabitation tends to be a serious issue is if the dog has a strong prey drive. In this case, there could be a real danger to your cat, and you need to be extremely careful.

HELP YOUR CAT, HELP YOURSELF

As you now know, providing your cat with as close to a stress-free and active lifestyle as possible is paramount to their health and longevity. Positive social interactions with others (cats and/or humans), coupled with appropriate amounts of exercise, promote a healthy body and mind, and both are necessary to achieve a longer life span for our cats. The bonus that comes with providing this idyllic, wonderful life for your cat is that you get to live longer too!

Your interactions with your kitty have proven human health benefits. A study by the *Journal of Vascular and Interventional Neurology* reported decreased levels of all cardiovascular deaths, including heart attack and stroke, among cat owners.[7] In addition to decreased mortality rates, pet ownership is also associated with improved cognitive function in geriatric adults.[8] Just like with our cats, a longer life span is only worthwhile when it comes along with good health, and your kitty can contribute to that.

Another major benefit of cat ownership is that it makes us happier as people. Trackinghappiness.com surveyed more than 12,000 people and found that pet owners are happier than non–pet owners.[9] And when scientists evaluated changes in life span associated with happiness, they found that optimistic people have an almost 15 percent increase in life span.[10] So, overall, it would appear that cat ownership creates a synergistic relationship resulting in longevity for both cat and human!

* * *

If you stop reading this book right now, you already have the necessary tools to make a significant improvement in your cat's life span and health span. Optimizing diet, exercise, and lifestyle is the lowest-hanging fruit in our quest for longevity and represents the changes that have the potential to make some of the greatest impacts. They also happen to be some of the easiest and most accessible ones you can make yourself—and they're good for *you* too!

I cannot stress this enough: Whatever you do to promote longevity in your cat, it must occur alongside the triad of optimized diet, exercise, and lifestyle. As we endeavor to help our cats live longer, better lives, no medical intervention on the horizon will make up for a lack of any one of these things, never mind all three. Ultimately, we are constructing a framework to dramatically extend the life span of our cats. The first step in any construction project is laying the foundation. It has to be solidly built, or nothing you place on top of it will last. The foundation for longevity is optimizing your cat's body and mind by providing the nutrients, activity, and social interactions their body evolved not only to survive but also to thrive on. By starting here, we are making sure that the biological machine that is your cat functions to the best of its ability. With that accomplished, we are then free to begin making adjustments to that machine that will result in better performance and an even longer life span, which is what we'll explore in Part III.

PART III

A HOLISTIC APPROACH

CHAPTER 5

UTILIZING ALLOPATHIC MEDICINE

Understanding the mechanics of the processes that lead to aging provides the backdrop for you to be able to take active steps to promote longevity. With the longevity-specific benefits of diet, exercise, and lifestyle now in your arsenal, it's time to look at the kinds of medical care your cat is receiving.

Let's begin with two truths about veterinary medicine. First, all veterinarians practice medicine with the primary goal of taking the best care of their patients. We certainly can, and will, examine some of the ways these good intentions might pave the road to you-know-where, but realize that even when things go wrong, there is no malice or hidden agenda in veterinary practice. I know of no other profession with more sincere, hardworking people than vet med.

The second truth is less optimistic. The pharmaceutical, research, and medical-education community is biased. Medical research costs money (a lot of it), and as such, it is driven toward avenues that optimize potential profits. Universities, which we would like to think are impartial research institutions, function in large part due to grants and endowments from Big Pharma. This relationship sometimes not only leads to a bias in what research is conducted but also may impact the conclusions researchers publish. It will therefore come as no surprise to you that the entire medical system is impartiality challenged.

All doctors, veterinarians and physicians alike, are educated within this murky environment, and our education is extremely parochial. Students are indoctrinated with the message that the only "real" medicine is taught through the institution, and ideas that come from other sources are not to be trusted. As a practical matter, this means veterinary students, and ultimately veterinarians, are instructed not to believe anything that doesn't come from the mainstream medical community—which, as we have just discussed, has a real problem with impartiality.

When you combine these two realities, the product is hardworking and sincere veterinarians with a bias they are likely unaware of and a medical system designed to reinforce that bias by promoting products and procedures that benefit Big Pharma. It makes for a tricky landscape for both veterinarians and cat owners interested in considering other options.

Despite all of this, it bears recognizing the good that Big Pharma does. Many of us would not be alive today without the benefits of vaccines, antibiotics, and modern medical procedures. The average life expectancy for a person in the U.S. today is about 77 years. In 1900, it was 47. One of the most significant factors giving us an extra 30 years of life is improvements in health care. The same is true for our cats. Yes, the system is flawed and we need to look at it with a somewhat critical eye, but turning our back on allopathic medicine is arguably even more counterproductive than trusting everything the medical system says without question. The best way to leverage allopathic medical care for the purposes of longevity is to take advantage of all the good while sidestepping the practices that either may directly cause harm or could negatively impact aging in the long term. So, let's take a look at what is being recommended and why, including vaccinations, surgical procedures, parasite prevention, dental care, and various drugs.

VACCINATION

The topic of vaccination has become controversial lately, particularly in the age of COVID. In some circles, *vaccine* seems to have become a dirty word. The truth is, vaccines save lives, and if our goal is longevity, protecting your cat against deadly diseases is a great place to start. However, vaccines can also cause a lot of harm. The key is knowing which to use and when.

There are multiple diseases cats *can* be vaccinated for, although no cat should be vaccinated for everything under the sun. The decision to vaccinate or not should hinge on five factors:

1. Is there a realistic chance the cat will be exposed to the disease?
2. If the cat gets the disease, how likely is it to do significant harm?
3. Does the cat already have immunity to the disease—in other words, have they already been given a vaccine that confers long-term immunity and therefore don't need a booster?

4. Are there legal or other regulatory requirements for the vaccine?
5. Is the cat going somewhere, such as a boarding facility, that requires vaccines?

Let's review the various vaccines offered for cats and consider how to best utilize them to promote longevity.*

Panleukopenia

Panleukopenia is a disease that can be deadly in kittens. Panleukopenia results from infection by a parvovirus specific to cats that causes severe gastrointestinal disease, including symptoms of diarrhea (frequently bloody), vomiting, and a whole host of secondary issues that are often fatal if not treated. The big challenge with panleukopenia is that the virus itself is incredibly hardy. It spreads through diarrhea from infected cats (generally kittens) and can remain infectious in the environment for up to six months. This means there is a very real chance your kitty could come in contact with this virus somewhere if they have been in a shelter environment or if they are going outside (another good reason to keep your cats indoors). If they are not protected when they get exposed, it could lead to an extremely sick kitten.

Panleukopenia vaccines are pretty much always administered in combination with other vaccines, usually referred to as *FVRCP*. The *P* is for panleukopenia. Feline viral rhinotracheitis, *FVR*, and calicivirus, *C*, are both highly contagious respiratory viruses. It should be noted rhinotracheitis and calicivirus are rarely fatal, but severe infections in kittens can lead to damage to their nasal passages and sinuses that might result in lifelong upper-respiratory problems.

* For specific detailed descriptions of the diseases that vaccines protect against and vaccine protocols, particularly for kittens, please see Appendix B of *The Ultimate Pet Health Guide*.

The long and the short of it is, you have to vaccinate kittens for panleukopenia and, by association, rhinotracheitis and calicivirus. If you don't, you are placing them at grave risk of getting a deadly disease. Even if your cat lives strictly indoors, vaccinating them as kittens will give them protection should they ever get outside accidentally. It's not that uncommon for a cat to occasionally slip outside through a door or window that was left open. For cats that go to a boarding facility, FVRCP is frequently required. Additionally, should there be a natural disaster where evacuation becomes necessary, cats can sometimes end up in temporary shelters or other environments where diseases can spread easily.

Feline Leukemia (FeLV)

FeLV is a virus that can cause immune suppression and, as the name would imply, occasionally leukemia (cancer). The disease is usually spread by direct contact with other cats through bites or scratches. It can, however, potentially be transmitted through saliva, meaning that shared food and water bowls can be a source of infection. The disease can also be transmitted from mothers to their kittens, making it very important to test kittens from feral or unknown parents prior to bringing them into a house with other cats who are FeLV-negative.

There is some debate among veterinarians as to the necessity of vaccinating kittens for FeLV if they are going to be strictly indoor cats. Unlike panleukopenia, which can be transmitted within the environment, or rhinotracheitis/calici, which are airborne, FeLV transmission usually requires close contact between cats. If there is any chance a kitten may be spending time outdoors, a FeLV vaccine is a good idea. If you are committed to your kitten being strictly indoors, it is probably something you can safely skip.

One thing to note about FeLV, and a similar virus called feline immunodeficiency virus (FIV), is that infected cats often do not show symptoms for years after infection. This means an infected cat can be living (indoors or outdoors) with a potentially deadly infectious disease and spreading it to others before anyone knows they are sick. Clearly, I have already made my point about the importance of keeping cats indoors. When it comes to cats with known FeLV or FIV, however, this is even more critical, because these cats are endangering every other cat they encounter when outside. Knowingly allowing a FeLV- or FIV-positive cat to continue to go outside is irresponsible, to say the least.

> There used to be a vaccine for FIV, but it was discontinued in the U.S. and Canada in 2015. The vaccine was not highly effective, and vaccinated cats could test "positive" for FIV for years after being vaccinated, making accurate diagnosis difficult.

Rabies

Rabies is a disease that you absolutely don't want your cat to get. It is 100 percent fatal and is transmissible to humans. Rabies is transmitted through a bite or scratch from an infected animal. The virus propagates in nerves and works its way up to the brain, where it causes fatal brain damage. Cats with rabies have cognitive abnormalities and may show unprovoked aggression or be mentally dull. The prevalence of rabies varies with geographic location, and rabies vaccination for dogs is legally required everywhere in the U.S. and most of the world. Some places legally require cats to be vaccinated for rabies and some don't, so check with your veterinarian to find out if there is a legal requirement for your kitty to get a rabies vaccine where you live.

Because of the severity of the disease and its ability to be transmitted to people, I usually vaccinate kittens for rabies so that if they get out at some point, they have a degree of protection. I like to wait until they are at least six months old, although vaccination can be done as early as four months. Waiting allows them to get a bit bigger and allows their immune system to mature. For strictly indoor cats, I don't generally recommend booster rabies vaccinations.

How Do Vaccines Work?

Vaccines, by design, cause inflammation, which stimulates the immune system and creates antibodies prepared to attack the disease in question should the cat be exposed. We've already discussed the impacts that inflammation has on longevity, so it stands to reason we would like to limit the amount and duration of inflammation in the body. The first step in limiting vaccine-induced inflammation is to not give too many vaccines at the same time. Ideally, cats should be given no more than one at a time, and allowing a month between necessary vaccines is a good idea.

One important fact the vaccine manufacturers won't tell you is that most vaccines last far longer than what it says on the label. This is particularly true for rabies. In many cases, cats that were properly vaccinated as kittens will carry immunity to rabies for a lifetime without subsequent boosters.

Keeping your cat indoors basically eliminates almost all disease-transmission risks. For reasons previously described, I do recommend vaccinating kittens at least for FVRCP and rabies. When they are one year old and "due" for boosters,

I generally don't give them if the cat is strictly indoors. Remember, one of the considerations when it comes to vaccines is to determine the risk of exposure. When they are indoors, their exposure approaches zero.

One possible exception with indoor cats is if they have access to a deck, terrace, or some other outdoor environment. Every now and again, I hear someone tell me a story about a bat that crash-landed. Bats are a source of rabies, and any bat on the ground is probably sick. I know this sounds far-fetched, but it happens! So if your cat has *any* outdoor access, even in a fenced yard, you might consider keeping them up to date on a rabies vaccine. You could also periodically run a rabies titer, which will let you know if they have sufficient antibodies from previous vaccination to protect them.

What Should I Be Concerned About?

When it comes to vaccines, there are two specific concerns: The first is a vaccine reaction. This is an allergic hypersensitivity to one or more of the components in a given vaccine. Symptoms can include facial swelling, hives, vomiting, and diarrhea. In rare cases, a life-threatening reaction called anaphylaxis causes a drop in blood pressure and restricts breathing. To the pharmaceutical industry's credit, the quality of vaccines has dramatically improved in the last 20 years, and vaccine reactions these days are rare.

The other concern is a little vaguer but potentially more dangerous. The vaccine inflammatory response can be achieved by a number of methods, including using modified, noninfectious live virus in the vaccine or using killed virus along with inflammatory compounds known as adjuvants. Adjuvants frequently contain metals such as mercury or aluminum.

There is a diagnosis in cats known as a vaccine-associated sarcoma, or injection-site sarcoma. As the name would imply, this is a cancer that occurs at the site of injection. It is thought these sarcomas occur in response to a chronic inflammatory process set up by one or more injections at a given location on the kitty. Research indicates the incidence of these tumors is somewhere between 1 in 10,000 and 1 in 30,000 vaccinations.[1]

The bad news is that these sarcomas are an aggressive form of cancer that requires surgery and frequently postsurgical radiation therapy. Sometimes, even after all this, they return. On the good side, over my career as a veterinarian, I have seen the incidence of these sarcomas drop dramatically. This is due, in part, to a change in vaccine strategy by veterinarians. When I was just starting out, a lot of cats were being vaccinated annually, and we used to give all vaccinations to cats in the same place—between their shoulder blades. Invariably, this is where the sarcomas appeared. It is likely that the repeated injection of inflammatory compounds in the same area year after year led to tumor formation.

I know what you are thinking: *Duh, it's so obvious that was a bad idea!* Of course, you are right, and hindsight is always 20/20. The truth is, no one knew it was going to be a problem. Now, most cats are no longer being vaccinated for everything every year, and for indoor cats, they may not be vaccinated at all after their kitten series. Additionally, veterinarians are now giving vaccines in different locations. For example, many vets give the FVRCP vaccine in the left front leg, FeLV in the left hind leg, and rabies in the right hind leg. Locations may vary from one vet to the next, but the point is to not continue to pound one site on the cat over and over again.

The credit for the other positive change with injection-site sarcomas lies with the vaccine companies. Over the years, they have done a good job cleaning up vaccines. They have been able to remove a lot of extraneous material and really purify them down to the necessary components that cause less inflammation and still get the job done. The combination of better products being given less often and at different areas on the cat has definitely led to decreases in these sarcomas. All that said, I stand by my philosophy of vaccinating animals only for what they need and only for as long as it takes to achieve immunity, and then no more.

Pet Insurance

Within the chapters of this book, a lot of discussion focuses on preventive care and promoting longevity through keeping pets healthy. All of this is critically important information. We do have to recognize that at some point your pet will get sick or possibly injured. When that occurs, the medical care necessary to restore your furry family member back to health is likely to get expensive. These days, emergency care for a very sick pet can climb into the tens of thousands of dollars quickly. Unlike human health care, there is no social safety net to guarantee treatment for the uninsured. More often than not, the end result of a pet with a curable condition whose owner cannot afford treatment is euthanasia. This is, without question, the most heartbreaking experience a pet owner or veterinarian can have.

When people find themselves in these situations, there are options. They can put the charge on a credit card or apply for credit through a service that is specifically designed for medical care, such as CareCredit. Please realize, your veterinarian is unlikely to be able to help with the costs. Veterinary medicine, like it or not, is a business that has to pay its employees, the expenses for drugs and supplies, rent, and so forth. I've owned veterinary hospitals for 20 years, and believe me, if we can help, we will. But if we routinely discounted or waived fees when people had financial hardships, we would go out of business.

The solution to all of this is pet insurance. I recommend pet insurance to every new client and for every new pet I see. Pet insurance can help defray some of the most expensive medical bills for animals. As is the case with human insurance, there are variables such as deductibles, exclusions for preexisting conditions (no Obamacare for pets), coverage limits, and so on. There are also some policies that cover alternative care, such as acupuncture and other holistic or complementary therapies. I strongly recommend thinking about what you want out of a policy. In other words, do you want a low deductible and higher premiums, or vice versa? Then do some Internet research and look at the policies offered by the many companies out there and read online reviews of those you are considering. The best plan is to obtain pet insurance early, before your pet has any significant medical history. This way, there will be no concerns about preexisting conditions that are not covered.

I cannot stress enough the degree to which pet insurance saves lives and allows for better care. From a longevity perspective, securing a good policy for your pet is one of the most impactful things you can do to support their health.

SPAY AND NEUTER

The term *spay* most commonly refers to a surgical procedure called an ovariohysterectomy in which the ovaries and uterus of a female cat are removed. *Neuter*, also known as an orchiectomy or castration, is when the testicles of a male cat are removed. These procedures are performed routinely in cats across the U.S. for population control and to decrease behavioral problems.

I'm just going to be very up-front here. Unless you are breeding purebreds, you do not want an adult intact cat in your house. Intact males, called *tomcats*, can develop a habit of urine spraying. I don't just mean peeing outside the box. I mean urinating horizontally onto your walls and furniture. And if you think regular cat pee smells bad, give tomcat urine a try. Setting aside any temperament issues with an intact male cat, such as aggression toward people or other animals, the urine issue should be enough to advocate for neutering.

When it comes to intact females, known as *queens*, urine spraying is not so much an issue, but their heat cycle certainly is. Cats are induced ovulators. This means that, unlike humans, they won't ovulate unless they are mating, and they will cycle in and out of heat (the time when they can become pregnant) until they are bred or spayed. If you haven't heard a cat in heat vocalize, it kind of sounds like someone is torturing a small animal. It's loud and persistent. And both toms and queens will constantly be looking for a way to get out of your house when they are ready to breed. Hormones are powerful motivators.

In cats, there is no reason to hesitate to spay or neuter. And when it comes to behaviors like urine spraying, they can become learned, meaning that even after you neuter toms, they might still do it. Thus, for both behavioral and population-control reasons, I strongly recommend that all cats be spayed or neutered. While many shelters and rescue groups will do this very early, my recommendation is to wait until they are around six months old. At this age, they are larger and better able to handle anesthesia but still young enough to not have gone into heat or developed any behavioral issues.

PARASITE PREVENTION

If you have a strictly indoor cat, parasite prevention should be minimal, as their exposure is also minimal. Depending on where you live, possible candidates for preventives include heartworm disease, gastrointestinal parasites, and fleas and ticks. Like everything else, the most advantageous use of these medications depends on your individual cat's situation.

Heartworm Disease

Heartworm disease is much more prevalent in dogs than it is in cats, but of all the parasites that cats can get, heartworms unquestionably have the deadliest consequences. The disease is exactly what it sounds like: your cat gets worms that live in their heart (as well as their lungs and blood vessels). Heartworm disease leads to heart and lung damage and, if untreated, is fatal. In fact, the treatment for heartworm disease in and of itself can be fatal, so proper prevention is critical.

Heartworms are transmitted by mosquitoes. When a mosquito infected with heartworm bites your cat, it leaves behind larval heartworms, who get to work on becoming adult worms. Within a couple of months, these worms take up residence in the bloodstream, heart, lungs, and blood vessels and begin to cause damage over a period of years.

Heartworm prevention involves giving your cat a drug called ivermectin or a similar drug in the same class. Products such as Heartgard and Interceptor utilize ivermectin and are labeled to be given monthly to prevent the larval-stage heartworms from maturing into adult worms.

There is another possible side effect of ivermectin. The drug is antibacterial and has been shown to cause changes in the microbiome in both animals and humans.[2] As we have already discussed, gut health is intimately associated with whole-body health and longevity. Though you're probably aware that indiscriminate use of antibiotics is a bad idea for gut health, you may not realize that a monthly dose of heartworm preventive could be having similar effects that might include GI upset or medical conditions associated with immune system imbalance.[3, 4]

When we take a hard look at the cost-benefit analysis of heartworm preventive versus heartworm infection, we first have to consider environmental factors. Is heartworm disease prevalent where you live? This is mostly a factor of climate and the presence of mosquitoes. Warmer, more humid climates like the southeastern portions of the U.S. have very high rates of heartworm disease. Where I live on the West Coast, rates are much lower because the climate is more temperate and drier, thus fewer mosquitoes. Interestingly, the areas of higher incidence of heartworm disease are spreading on the map, most likely due to the overall climate getting warmer. The American Heartworm Society maintains maps of the incidence of heartworm disease across the country that you can find on their website.

The reality is, most cats don't need heartworm preventives, especially if they live indoors. If you live in a heartworm-endemic area, the incidence of heartworm disease in cats is higher than elsewhere. And while it is certainly possible for mosquitoes to get into your house, the exposure rate for strictly indoor cats even in these areas is limited. But, if you live somewhere with a high heartworm rate, speak with a holistic veterinarian in your area and see what they recommend. Outside of these situations, it is probably not necessary.

Gastrointestinal Parasites

Gastrointestinal parasites include a variety of worms (gross!) such as roundworms, hookworms, whipworms, and tapeworms. Cats can also get microbial parasites like giardia. It isn't important to cover the specifics of each of these conditions other than to say it is better if your cat doesn't have parasites.

Most parasites are contracted through fecal-oral transmission, meaning your cat was nosing around poop or someplace on the ground where poop had been, and they ingested parasite eggs. The one notable exception to this is tapeworms, which are contracted when your cat eats a flea. As is the case with heartworm disease, strictly indoor cats will have very limited (if any) exposure to parasites. The biggest parasite risk is tapeworms, because fleas can get inside your house. Most parasites, including tapeworms, are easily treated with medication. This is one of those times when a pharmaceutical is the best solution, since treatment is usually quick and effective. It is always a good idea to run a stool test annually to make sure your cat is clear of parasites. If you live somewhere warm and humid and your cat is spending time outside, consider testing every six months.

Fleas and Ticks

Fleas and ticks are a different story than heartworm disease or gastrointestinal parasites. Fleas, in general, are largely a nuisance more than anything else. In warm and humid climates, severe flea infestations can be life-threatening, but this is rare and usually only occurs in very small or very sick animals. As mentioned, fleas can also transmit tapeworms, but these are easily treatable and do not generally cause serious disease.

Unlike most infectious diseases and parasites, your indoor cat is not totally off the hook when it comes to fleas. It's actually not that uncommon to see indoor cats with fleas. They can come in on your dog or even on your shoes or clothing. Once they are inside, fleas are happy to live there. The weather is always nice, your pets provide an easily available food source, and your carpet and furniture make a wonderful place to live and to hatch eggs.

The good news about flea control is that you can use it as needed. Flea populations decrease dramatically when it is cold, but remember, it is never winter inside your house. If you have a population of fleas reproducing in your home, you've got some work to do that will probably involve treating both the cat and the house for four to six months to break the life cycle.

Ticks are more problematic than fleas, because they can transmit diseases such as Lyme, hemotrophic mycoplasmosis, and anaplasmosis, among others. Interestingly, tickborne diseases such as these do not always cause visible illness in cats. Chronic infection, however, can set up long-term inflammation and potentially trigger autoimmune disease, both of which are definitely not conducive to a long and healthy life. Another thing to remember about tick control is that it is not only about your cat's health.

Tick issues in cats are less common than in dogs because cats are such fastidious groomers. Also—and I know I am repeating myself—your indoor cat will have almost no tick exposure, unless your dog brings one in or you happen to have one on your shoe or clothing. As a rule, tick control is rarely needed for indoor cats, but it is something to consider if the cat is going outside, depending on the environment and the season. One other note regarding tickborne disease: while it may not affect cats dramatically, Lyme is an absolutely devastating disease in humans, and if your outdoor cat is bringing ticks home, you are at risk as well.

Unlike with heartworm preventives, there are a lot of options out there when it comes to flea and tick control. They include topicals, collars, and sprays. Each has its pros and cons when it comes to efficacy and impact on longevity, and like all other medications, they should be used only when needed.

Topical products and flea collars both repel and kill the fleas and ticks, so they offer the benefit of not necessitating being bitten in order for the flea or tick to be exposed and die. In addition to your cat avoiding getting bitten, it also means, if you have an outdoor cat, they are less likely to carry insects/arachnids home that could get on you and your furniture. The flip side, of course, is that topical flea and tick products are chemicals on your cat's coat that you will come into contact with. In both humans and cats, exposure can cause rare side effects like skin irritation, gastrointestinal upset, and potentially even neurologic complications.

The other flea-and-tick option for your cat is natural sprays, usually composed of essential oils. When used as directed, these products are very safe. They are effective at repelling, and even potentially killing, fleas and ticks, although they will never be as dramatically effective as their pharmaceutical cousins. Natural sprays can be a great option when the fleas and ticks aren't too bad. You can google "flea and tick incidence map" to see what your area is like, although if you have had your cat for any period of time, you probably already know from experience. Choosing what kind of prevention to use is a cost-benefit analysis hinging on the amount of exposure your cat has to fleas and ticks (if any). Regardless of the product, just remember that less is more.

DENTAL CARE

Just as your dentist is constantly reminding you, dental health is critically important to overall health, and that applies to cats too. Evidence in both dogs and humans shows that good dental hygiene is correlated with a longer life span, and there is every reason to extend this to cats.[5, 6]

Good dental health for your cat starts at home. Regular tooth brushing, ideally daily, is the single best thing you can do to keep your cat's teeth healthy and supportive of their longevity. You can get a cat-specific toothbrush or, if you have a larger cat, a very small toothbrush meant for people. Toothpaste for cats is mostly about flavor in order to make the experience interesting—that can be really useful for a cat who doesn't like the brush in their mouth! When you brush, concentrate your efforts along the gumline and outer surfaces of the teeth since that is where most issues occur. You will have to train your cat to accept tooth brushing, just like with anything else. Start slowly and be very gentle. If it hurts, they aren't going to give you a second chance. Whether you can brush every day or not, you might consider supplementing with dental chews, oral rinses, and so forth. When it comes to chews and rinses, I strongly encourage you to use only all-natural products.

We want to limit your cat's environmental toxin exposure, and giving them dental treats with antibacterial chemicals is not ideal.

Regardless of how diligent you are with oral hygiene at home, your cat is going to need their teeth professionally cleaned from time to time. In my office, we like to augment home dental care with periodic nonanesthetic dental cleanings. These procedures do not take the place of a full cleaning under anesthesia, but they can help with spots you are missing with your home care. Nonanesthetic dentals should only be performed in veterinary offices under the direct supervision of a veterinarian. It is quite common to find dental problems during these procedures that necessitate a consultation, dental X-rays, and a full cleaning under anesthesia.

What to Do When Your Cat Resists Tooth Brushing

Unquestionably, tooth brushing is the "gold standard" for keeping your cat's teeth clean. But let's be honest, sometimes tooth brushing is easier said than done. We are all busy people, and not everyone is able to set aside the time for regular tooth brushing for their pet. Not to mention that it's not necessarily the favorite pastime of our cats, either!

While some dental home care is going to be better than none, we do need to consider the best alternative options outside of brushing (please keep trying). Dental chews, oral rinses, and additives to your cat's water bowl can all be helpful. Since dental care is an ongoing, lifelong process, however, we must consider the potential long-term effects of dental-care products. Many such products for animals contain chemicals like chlorhexidine and sodium hexametaphosphate. While there is no definitive evidence of negative long-term health impacts associated with these compounds, my preference is to "keep it natural" whenever possible. There are natural dental-care products on the market for cats that utilize algae, enzymes, curcumin, and other ingredients that will help keep teeth clean when used regularly. Products such as these are a great addition to your cat's home dental-care plan. That said, please try to brush as often as possible.

ANTIBIOTICS

As a class of drugs, antibiotics are unquestionably lifesaving, and many of us (and our cats) would not be alive today if not for access to drugs to control bacterial infections. And a major reason for the extra three decades of life humans enjoy on average today is that we rarely die of bacterial diseases.

So, I am not debating the efficacy and usefulness of antibiotics—but they can also lead to serious problems. The most direct concern is what these medications are doing to the microbiome. So what happens when you disrupt the normal gut flora through the use of antibiotics? It depends both on the duration of the course of antibiotics and on the age of the human or cat taking the medication. In humans, long-term use of antibiotics in older patients is associated with increased all-cause mortality.[7] While we don't have the same studies in cats, it is reasonable to suspect that disruption in the gut biome is going to have negative impacts similar to those seen in humans.

Antibiotics are prescribed far too liberally in veterinary medicine. In many cases, oral antibiotics are used for conditions that can be treated in other ways, such as minor skin infections, or for diseases that don't respond to antibiotics, such as viral infections. The allopathic paradigm is to use antibiotics as if they don't have any negative side effects. As an integrative practitioner, I do sometimes prescribe antibiotics for my patients. However, I always begin by looking for an alternative, and if I have to use antibiotics, I make sure to put the cat on a prebiotic and probiotics during and for at least 30 days after the course of medication, as dysbiosis, or an imbalance in the microbiome, can have both short- and long-term effects, including diarrhea, vomiting, and more systemic immune system imbalance. If your veterinarian wants to put your cat on antibiotics, respectfully ask if there is another option or if it is okay to try something else first. There are going to be times when antibiotics are a necessity, but in many cases, other options may be available. The bottom line: use antibiotics if they are absolutely necessary, but avoid them whenever possible.

STEROIDS

Another commonly used class of drugs in veterinary medicine is steroids. Steroids perfectly embody the metaphor of the double-edged sword. They are the best and the worst drugs in the world, all at the same time. Steroids are, unquestionably, the best anti-inflammatory drugs known to medical science, and there are times when their use saves lives. The best way to think about steroids is that they can be great for short-term use to treat severe medical conditions. Things become a lot murkier when they are continued for the longer term, such as months or years. Long-term side effects of steroids include immune suppression, muscle loss, and negative impacts on the liver, and they can lead to diabetes in cats. While there are circumstances where longer-term steroids may be necessary, such as with severe autoimmune disease, they must be used with caution, and every effort should be taken to wean patients off these medications at the earliest opportunity. Steroids should never be used long term for noncritical conditions such as allergies.

* * *

When used appropriately, allopathic medicine is highly beneficial and promotes longevity. The problem, of course, is Western medicine tends to overuse these methods because they are the only tools in the toolbox. As with everything in life, balance is the key to success, and the most advantageous way to utilize allopathic medicine to promote longevity is by balancing its use with natural supplements.

CHAPTER 6

SUPPLEMENTS

Supplements are any substance taken to provide extra nutrients to augment your cat's diet. Ideally, they originate from natural sources, although in some cases they can be synthetically created. Supplements come in different forms: capsule, tablet, powder, or liquid. I talk with a lot of people about which supplements are right for their cat, and the key to supplementation for longevity is to keep an eye on which of the hallmarks of aging any given supplement addresses and create a regimen that addresses as many as possible.

Since frequently the patients I see have serious medical conditions, like cancer, organ failure, and autoimmune disease, the strategy for supplementation hinges on how to best address what is going on with the individual cat. When it comes to general longevity, however, there are a core set of supplements that almost every cat will benefit from. Beyond that, the individualized nature of medicine comes into play.

If you google "supplements for longevity," you will receive about 17 million hits—I just tried it. Even if you could snap your fingers and instantly eliminate all the redundancy and general Internet garbage, you would still be left with an incredibly long list of supplements that have legitimate positive effects on longevity. So how are you supposed to know which ones are best to give your cat? In this chapter I will outline my recommended supplements, explain how they can have a positive effect on the hallmarks of aging, and discuss whether they should be taken periodically or long term.

THE AMAZING VERSATILITY OF SUPPLEMENTS

Countless times in my career I have seen a cat for a chronic problem that allopathic medicine has not been able to resolve. Whether it is arthritis, cancer, gastrointestinal disease, skin issues, or anything else, it's really a question of providing the pet with something their body needs to help it heal itself.

Oftentimes with healthy animals you don't see dramatic changes when you begin supplementation because, largely, we are trying to maintain their level of good health. With sick pets, though, the improvements can be surprising.

I see many dogs and cats whose owners and veterinarians have exhausted the conventional therapy options for arthritis, and their pet is still in pain. Sometimes, the medications these pets can take are limited due to concerns about side effects, such as kidney, liver, or gastrointestinal complications. Utilizing natural anti-inflammatory and pain-relieving supplements—for example, boswellia, curcumin, fish oil, and others—can make a life-changing difference in these animals. Not only do supplements such as these have positive impacts all on their own, but they can also almost always be used in conjunction with pharmaceuticals—and they even have the ability to mitigate some of the side effects of the pharmaceuticals, such as protecting liver function.

SUPPLEMENT OPTIONS

The 30-plus supplements presented in this chapter are my top picks for availability, safety, and effectiveness, according to the information we have right now. Please note that for most of the supplements listed here, there is no feline-specific research. They are used regularly for people interested in their own longevity, and while many are not commonly given to cats, my clinical experience and knowledge of feline physiology tells me they are safe at the dosages noted. (Even so, I always recommend consulting with your veterinarian before starting any supplement or medication for your cat.) Plenty of other supplements out there successfully promote longevity, so there's no way this could be a complete list, but it is a great place to start. Plus, now that you are familiar with the hallmarks of aging, you will know what to look for when you encounter something not on this list.

Given the lack of regulation in the supplement industry, it can be a challenge for pet owners to source high-quality supplements. As consumers, we all must do our due diligence when choosing supplements for our pets . . . and ourselves. When it comes to pet-specific supplements, the National Animal Supplement Council (NASC) is an organization that evaluates supplements to make sure they are made well and contain what they say they contain. You can be sure products with the NASC seal are high quality. For pet products that don't have the NASC seal or supplements made for people, the best strategy is to do some research, look for reputable brands, and, when possible, get a brand recommendation from someone with knowledge about the supplement in question.

The following supplements are categorized alphabetically and then presented in a chart, noting which of the original nine hallmarks of aging they help counter. Let me take a moment to acknowledge the obvious: medicating cats can be challenging, and natural medicine such as herbs often doesn't taste very good. If possible, pills or capsules can be a good option to avoid bitter or other tastes your cat finds offensive. Keep in mind that anything you plan to do for the sake of your cat's longevity has to be sustainable on your end, otherwise it is likely not going to be an effective long-term strategy. At the end of the chapter, we will discuss supplement strategies to obtain the best results while keeping in mind your commitment of time and effort.

Please note that you will not be giving your cat every single one of these supplements included in this chapter—I will offer advice on how to choose a few to focus on to promote your cat's longevity. Let's get started!

Ashwagandha

Withania somnifera, also known as ashwagandha, is an herb whose uses in traditional Indian medicine date back as far as 6000 B.C. Ashwagandha has long been used to promote longevity, and now with the benefit of modern scientific research, we understand why.

Ashwagandha is described as an *adaptogen*, or an herb that helps the body manage stress. More specifically, ashwagandha enhances telomerase activity, lengthening those important telomeres that protect chromosomes from damage.[1] It also addresses deregulated nutrient sensing by increasing AMPK and inhibiting mTOR, the proteins that help balance the body's response to food.[2, 3]

Dosing of ashwagandha varies depending on how the herb is processed. For unprocessed, granulated ashwagandha, give 1 gram twice daily. For extracted and dried preparations, give 250 to 500 milligrams twice daily. As a liquid extract, 0.5 to 1 milliliter can be given twice daily.

Berberine

Berberine is another herb that has been used in various forms of traditional medicine for thousands of years. It occurs in many plants, including goldenseal, Oregon grape, and barberry, among others. Berberine has positive effects on longevity through AMPK activation and by suppressing senescent cells—cells that, due to damage, no longer function properly—so that they don't negatively affect working cells.[4, 5]

Since berberine is a constituent of other herbs, there isn't a specific dosing level to give. You can give extracts of various berberine-containing herbs (where the levels of berberine will vary) and also products sold with concentrated berberine. For cats, the best source is an herbal extract (liquid, powder, or capsule) of a berberine-containing herb that is made for cats. Berberine is generally safe, and the most common side effect is GI upset. Fair warning, berberine is bitter, and giving it in a form your kitty can taste (such as a liquid) may be challenging.

Carotenoids

Carotenoids are a class of compounds produced by plants yellow, orange, and red in color. These are the things that give many fruits and vegetables their bright colors. Carotenoids such as beta-carotene (a precursor to vitamin A), lycopene, lutein, astaxanthin, zeaxanthin, and so forth are potent antioxidants and, when part of a dietary and supplement regimen, have an effect on improving immune function, as well as limiting genomic instability and certain types of cancer.[6]

Carotenoids are found in pet foods, although probably not in quantities sufficient to promote longevity in our cats.

As noted, there are a lot of carotenoids out there, and you don't have to supplement them all. The better plan would be to use a supplement containing multiple carotenoids and/or rotating through different ones over time. Dosing recommendations here are a little tricky, since it depends on which carotenoids you are considering. For example, I use astaxanthin at a dose of 1 to 2 milligrams per day to help with skin and coat, as well as overall inflammation levels. Similarly, you can use 10 milligrams of lycopene and 250 to 500 IU of beta-carotene per day.

CoQ10

Coenzyme Q10 (CoQ10), also known as ubiquinone, is naturally present in all animals and most bacteria. CoQ10 is an antioxidant and anti-inflammatory, and it plays a role in cellular energy generation. It has been shown to help control diabetes and improve cardiovascular, liver, and kidney function.[7] CoQ10 specifically supports mitochondrial function (providing energy to cells) and genomic stability (accurate replication of DNA), both combating important hallmarks of aging.[8]

CoQ10 is not water-soluble, which means it has to be given with a fatty meal or in a preparation that specifically makes it more absorbable. A good dosage for cats is about 10 milligrams per day.

Curcumin

If you are familiar at all with supplements for cats or humans, you are probably aware of curcumin. This yellow pigment is the active ingredient in the herb turmeric, and it possesses antioxidant, anti-inflammatory, and liver-protective properties. Interestingly, it also has properties that can reverse stem cell exhaustion and prevent genomic instability. In other words, curcumin can make older stem cells act younger and prevent errors in DNA replication.[9, 10, 11]

Curcumin is not particularly well absorbed by the GI tract, so simply feeding your cat (or yourself) turmeric will not have much effect. The absorption of curcumin can be increased by combining it with fat and black pepper (sometimes referred to as "golden paste"), but even then, it still isn't great. Successful supplementation with curcumin requires the use of a preparation specifically designed to be more bioavailable. This is frequently done by a process called microencapsulation, which makes the curcumin water-soluble and thus easily absorbable. Appropriate dosing of curcumin is highly dependent on the way it is produced, as different encapsulation processes have different effects. In this case, I would suggest finding a high-quality, highly absorbable product. If the product is for cats, follow the dosing instructions. If it is for humans, give no more than one-quarter of the recommended dose for people. You can give your cat this supplement every day.

EGCG

Epigallocatechin gallate (EGCG) is the component in green tea that makes it so good for you. EGCG is anti-inflammatory, and it has been shown to protect the brain and the heart. As a pro-longevity supplement, EGCG mitigates cellular senescence, mitochondrial dysfunction, epigenetic alterations, and deregulated nutrient sensing.[12, 13, 14, 15] A dose of 50 to 100 milligrams per day is about right for cats.

Essential Fatty Acids

In Chapter 2, we discussed the pro-longevity benefits of EPA and DHA, the essential fatty acids found in fish oil. The almost five-year increase in life span for people consuming fish oil is due to its effects on multiple hallmarks of aging, including reducing telomere attrition, mitochondrial dysfunction, deregulated nutrient sensing, and altered intercellular communication.[16, 17, 18, 19] If you are concerned about fish oil for environmental or other reasons, you can find supplements made from marine algae. Another essential fatty acid, alpha-linolenic acid (ALA), is found in nuts, seeds, and their associated oils. While ALA is not converted to EPA and DHA in cats as it is in humans, it has its own benefits, including suppressing genomic instability and mitochondrial dysfunction.[20, 21, 22]

There is a wide range of dosing recommendations for essential fatty acids. For the purposes of longevity, a good dose to start with would be about 150 milligrams of combined EPA and DHA. For ALA, use 20 milligrams per day. Omega-3 fatty acid levels can be measured in dogs (see Chapter 2), and I would anticipate this will be available for kitties soon. This will allow you to really know if your cat is getting enough essential fatty acids. The goal is to supplement so they test at the upper end of what is considered normal.

Fisetin

Fisetin is a compound that is found in various fruits and vegetables, such as strawberries, apples, persimmons, and cucumbers. Fisetin has been found to be a potent senolytic, meaning it can rid the body of senescent cells.[23] The dose of fisetin is 10 to 20 milligrams, and it should be used around two to three days per month to allow the body to "clean up" excessive senescent cells.

Magnesium

Magnesium came up in Chapter 2 during the discussion of diagnostic tests. This mineral plays a role in boosting energy metabolism and cell proliferation, while slowing apoptosis (programmed cell death), oxidative stress, and inflammation.[24] Magnesium is found in dark leafy greens, nuts, seeds, beans, and grains—depending on the food you give your cat, they may be getting enough magnesium in their diet.

Magnesium can be supplemented orally, although it has a tendency to cause GI upset. One option is to use it topically by rubbing a magnesium cream into bare skin for absorption. Since your cat may already be getting enough magnesium, hold off on supplementing magnesium until they are tested. Once you know their levels, you will know how much to supplement.

Melatonin

You might be familiar with melatonin as a supplement used as a sleep aid. Melatonin is also an antioxidant, and it has been shown to prevent cellular senescence. Interestingly, melatonin is produced in the gastrointestinal tract in response to intermittent fasting, which we already know has positive effects on longevity. There has been some speculation that one of the benefits of intermittent fasting is the production of melatonin, and it is possible that supplementing with melatonin may have similar effects.[25, 26] Melatonin is very safe and can be dosed at 1 milligram per day.

Mushrooms

Mushrooms are ubiquitous around the world and truly illuminate what people mean when they say "food as medicine." Mushrooms are known to have properties that help fight cancer, support the immune system, promote recycling of old cells (autophagy) and thus limit senescent cells, and the list goes on.[27] A recent study showed mushroom consumption in people decreased overall mortality during the study period by 16 percent.[28] Among the most powerful medicinal and longevity-promoting mushrooms are ganoderma (reishi), shiitake, chaga, turkey tail, and cordyceps, although there are many more. Some of these can be consumed as food, and some require their active ingredients to be extracted in alcohol or hot water or by other means.

Dosing of mushrooms for longevity varies based on the type of mushroom and/or the nature of the extract. The good news is at the end of the day, mushrooms are food, so they are very safe. If using a product made for animals, follow the directions. If you are using a human product, use one-quarter of the recommended dose for kitties.

An interesting note about mushrooms: they have an earthy, umami flavor that can be somewhat reminiscent of meat. I know veterinarians who started feeding their cats pieces of mushrooms when they were kittens, and now as adults, the cats search them out as treats!

N-Acetylcysteine

N-acetylcysteine (NAC) is derived from the amino acid cysteine and has several therapeutic uses in human and veterinary medicine, including helping break up mucus in the lungs and also treating toxicities such as acetaminophen (Tylenol), which is universally toxic in cats. As a longeity-promoting supplement, NAC has been shown to help reduce oxidative stress as well as address genomic instability and mitochondrial dysfunction.[29, 30] NAC can be dosed in cats between 50 and 100 milligrams twice daily.

NMN

Nicotinamide mononucleotide (NMN) is a precursor to nicotinamide adenine dinucleotide (NAD). NAD is a critical component of all cells in the body and plays a role in energy generation and cellular repair. NAD is thought to decrease the inflammation that accompanies and promotes aging (inflammaging).[31]

Since NAD is not effective when given orally, its precursor, NMN, is the next best thing. There is research evidence to suggest that NMN can reverse age-related conditions through stimulating the production of NAD.[32] NMN supplementation can be dosed between 25 and 50 milligrams per day.

Oleuropein Aglycone

Oleuropein aglycone is derived from olive oil and olive leaves. This fascinating compound has received a lot of attention for its potential benefits for people with Alzheimer's disease and dementia. It promotes cellular autophagy and thus helps the body rid itself of senescent and other damaged cells, as well as supporting proteostasis (the process that recycles misfolded proteins).[33, 34] It also prevents oxidative damage and has anti-inflammatory effects.

Products containing oleuropein aglycone are usually powdered olive leaves or olive leaf extract. For powdered olive leaves, give about ⅛ to ¼ teaspoon in food per day. Alternatively, give around 5 milligrams of an extract that contains at least 12 percent oleuropein.

Plasmalogens

Every cell in the body has a membrane that creates the boundary between inside and outside the cell. The cell membrane is largely made up of molecules called phospholipids, along with various receptors and channels within the membrane that allow for transfer of materials, cell signaling, and so forth. Plasmalogens are a form of phospholipid that occurs in all mammalian cell membranes, although it is found in the highest concentrations in the brain, red blood cells, and muscle tissue.[35] Plasmalogens appear to serve a critical purpose as antioxidants, and higher levels of plasmalogens are associated with neurotransmitter release, longevity, decreased inflammation, and improved cognitive function. They may also have value in the treatment of neurodegenerative diseases.[36, 37]

Plasmalogens show a lot of promise in the field of longevity medicine, although there have been no studies looking at their use in cats. That said, plasmalogen supplementation is safe and something you might want to consider if you have an aging cat, especially if there is some concern about their cognitive function. One of the most prominent researchers in the field of plasmalogen supplementation is Dr. Dayan Goodenowe, and you can purchase supplements through his website, www.prodrome.com. The supplements are not inexpensive, so only use them if you feel your cat really needs them. There isn't a known dose for cats, and I would recommend giving them one-quarter of the adult human dose.

Probiotics

Most of us are familiar with probiotics, which contain bacteria that are beneficial for gut health. The gut contains approximately 70 percent of the immune cells in the body, so gut health directly translates to overall health and longevity. An unhealthy microbiome is so detrimental to overall health that it is specifically labeled as one of the hallmarks of aging. In addition to protecting us from infections, cancer, and so forth, the immune system controls the body's level of inflammation, which is a factor in four of the hallmarks of aging: cellular senescence, altered intercellular communication, microbiome disturbance, and inflammation. The term *inflammaging* specifically describes how chronic inflammation promotes the aging process. Thus, it will come as no surprise that a healthier gut will help protect your cat from the effects of aging.

Without question, a healthier gut starts with nutrition in the form of a balanced, fresh, whole-food diet. The correct nutrients feed beneficial gut bacteria and limit the harmful ones. We can further improve these effects by utilizing probiotics for gut health, and research confirms probiotics play a role in limiting inflammation and aging.[38] Their potency is generally measured in "colony-forming units," or CFUs. Good-quality probiotics should report CFUs per serving in the billions. Other beneficial additions to probiotics are prebiotics (food for beneficial bacteria) and postbiotics (the beneficial components created by these bacteria). Pre- and postbiotics are sometimes added to probiotic supplements.

If your cat is eating a balanced, fresh, whole-food diet, they are likely getting enough prebiotics. Postbiotics are fatty acids such as medium-chain triglycerides found in some fats like coconut oil. A small amount of coconut oil can be added to your cat's diet—around ⅛ teaspoon per day. Dosing of probiotics is highly variable, depending on the product and the health status of your cat. There are strains of probiotics that are specifically for animals, but you can use a human product as well. You can certainly use an animal or human product off the shelf and see how it works, although you may be able to get some guidance from your veterinarian on how to select a formula right for your cat.

Pterostilbene

The class of compounds called polyphenols is commonly found in fruits, vegetables, teas, and spices. These micronutrients frequently have antioxidant properties. Pterostilbene is one such compound, and it is the main antioxidant component of blueberries. Pterostilbene has been shown to limit oxidative stress, inflammation, and aging in research models.[39] In addition, there is evidence it can play a role in the prevention and treatment of age-related cognitive decline, which is definitely an issue for some older cats.[40] Within the scope of the hallmarks of aging, pterostilbene promotes proteostasis. Misfolded proteins not only are nonfunctional but also can be a cause of significant disease and aging, so being able to refold or reuse these proteins has immense benefits.[41] Dosing of pterostilbene for a kitty would be around 25 milligrams per day.

Pycnogenol

Created from the bark of the French maritime pine tree, pycnogenol is a standardized extract that contains multiple flavonoids. These compounds are extracted from all kinds of plants and have natural antioxidant activity and have been shown to play a role in longevity through limiting inflammation, reducing oxidative stress, promoting circulation by keeping blood vessels healthy, and maintaining cognitive function.[42, 43, 44, 45] Anecdotally, pycnogenol has been reported to help animals with conditions ranging from allergies to arthritis and even cancer. Pycnogenol can be given to cats at a dose of 10 to 20 milligrams per day.

Quercetin

Quercetin is a flavonoid, like pycnogenol, and it possesses many of the same properties that keep the body healthy and promote longevity.[46] And quercetin has additional effects: it promotes proteostasis and may help reduce senescent cell burden.[47, 48, 49] In longevity-specific research, quercetin is frequently used along with the drug dasatinib to reduce senescent cell load. Dasatinib is a chemotherapy drug used to treat leukemia (see Chapter 7). Quercetin can be given to cats at a dose of 125 milligrams once daily on an empty stomach.

Resveratrol

Resveratrol is one of the more well-known longevity supplements. It is the main component of grape-seed extract, which has long been used to promote health and longevity. Resveratrol is a polyphenol and has many of the same positive effects previously discussed with regard to pterostilbene.[50] Resveratrol has also been shown to promote longevity through positive effects on multiple hallmarks of aging by regulating oxidative stress, energy metabolism, nutrient sensing, epigenetics, and apoptosis, and by improving mitochondrial dysfunction.[51, 52] As you can see, resveratrol can be a big player in the field of longevity supplements.

The active form of resveratrol is trans-resveratrol, and dosing should be determined by the trans-resveratrol content of a given supplement. Dosing is about 50 milligrams of trans-resveratrol per day.

Selenium

Selenium is an essential micronutrient, one of the enzymes and proteins in the body that help with the production of DNA and prevent cell damage and genomic instability.[53, 54] Like every other mineral we have discussed in this chapter, not having enough selenium in the body can be detrimental.

One particular fact to note about selenium is that too much is equally bad, and since selenium is usually dosed in very small amounts (micrograms), it is best to avoid using standalone selenium supplements, as there is a risk of toxicity. I strongly recommend supplementing only using a multivitamin that contains selenium. If you use a product made for animals, follow the directions on the label. If you are using a human supplement, consult with your veterinarian or a veterinary nutritionist for guidance.

Serine

Serine is an amino acid that is used by the body to create proteins, and like almost all amino acids, it occurs in both an L form and a D form. In the case of serine, both forms have positive effects on longevity, although from a supplementation perspective, we are focusing on L-serine. Serine is thought to regulate proteostasis and cellular senescence.[55] Serine is also neuroprotective, and there is evidence to support serine's use as a treatment for neurologic diseases such as ALS in humans.[56, 57] While cats don't get ALS, they can sometimes have decreased neurologic function as they age. Serine may also improve learning, memory, and immune system function. For longevity purposes, a good dose of serine should be about 0.5 milligram per pound of body weight per day.

Spermidine

It's not what it sounds like . . . sort of. Spermidine is a chemical compound found in plants such as soybeans, vegetables, and grains. Yes, it is also found in semen, but spermidine supplements are solely derived from plants, such as wheat-germ extract. (The germ is the reproductive part of the plant.) Setting aside the strange name, spermidine has been shown to extend life and have antiaging effects in laboratory animals and humans.[58] It improves mitochondrial function and proteostasis, induces autophagy, and acts as an anti-inflammatory and antioxidant.[59] Dose spermidine at 0.5 milligram once daily.

Sulforaphane

Sulforaphane is a compound derived from cruciferous vegetables such as broccoli. Research shows it affects genomic instability, deregulated nutrient sensing, proteostasis, and mitochondrial function. It also has antioxidant and anti-inflammatory effects, as well as anticancer activity.[60, 61] Dosing of sulforaphane for cats is in the range of 5 to 10 milligrams per day.

Vitamin A

The longevity effects of vitamin A are discussed in the "Carotenoids" section (page 125). There is no longevity-specific dose for vitamin A, but dosing of 2000 IU per pound of body weight has been shown to be safe, although probably higher than necessary. Consider 250 IU per day. Vitamin A is fat-soluble and should be given with food. Note that unlike most mammals, cats are unable to convert beta-carotene, a vitamin A precursor, to functional vitamin A, so they should be supplemented with "preformed" vitamin A rather than beta-carotene.[62]

Vitamin B

There are eight different types of B vitamins, and while we don't need to get into a detailed discussion of each, you should realize the scope of cellular and metabolic processes regulated in part by B vitamins. This family of vitamins plays a role in energy metabolism; DNA methylation, synthesis, and repair; and immune system function. Not surprisingly, deficiency in one or more of these vitamins can lead to problems, including dysfunction of mitochondria and the immune system, as well as inflammatory diseases and cognitive decline.[63] Two of the B vitamins, cobalamin (B_{12}) and folate, can be easily measured through a blood sample.

B vitamins are naturally found in foods like meat, liver and other organ meats, leafy greens, and so forth. Supplementation of B vitamins for cats is best done using an appropriately dosed multivitamin or B-complex preparation. If you get one made for animals, use the dose recommended on the label. B vitamins are water-soluble and you really can't do much harm, but you can certainly combine them with other vitamins, such as A and D. If you are using a multivitamin for humans, consult with your veterinarian or a veterinary nutritionist.

Vitamin C

Vitamin C is another vitamin with a wide range of antiaging effects. It limits oxidative stress, genomic instability, and telomere attrition, as well as modulating senescent cells and inflammaging.[64, 65] Intravenous vitamin C in high doses is also used by integrative and functional medicine practitioners for the treatment of cancer patients. Like the B vitamins, vitamin C is water-soluble and, other than the potential for gastrointestinal upset, there are no realistic concerns about overdosing. Natural sources of vitamin C include a wide variety of fruits and vegetables, including citrus, bell peppers, tomatoes, broccoli, and so forth.

Vitamin C can be supplemented in many different forms such as ascorbic acid, Ester-C, liposomal vitamin C, vitamin C with rosehips, and so forth. The dosing will vary depending on the type of supplement being used. The most common form of vitamin C is ascorbic acid, and the dose of that is 125 milligrams per day. Doses can be split twice daily, which may limit the chance of GI upset if your cat has a sensitive tummy. For other forms of vitamin C, use the dose recommended for products made for animals, or consult with your veterinarian or a veterinary nutritionist if using a product made for humans.

Vitamin D

One of the major functions of vitamin D is the regulation of calcium and phosphorus in the body. Low levels of vitamin D can lead to decreased calcium absorption. In humans, this is a contributing factor to osteoporosis, a weakening and fragility of the bones. While we don't see this phenomenon in cats, vitamin D also plays a role in the prevention of sarcopenia, or loss of muscle tissue.[66] Poor muscle mass is something commonly encountered in older cats, and it can contribute significantly to deteriorating quality of life as a result of decreased mobility and joint pain. Vitamin D also helps regulate immune system function and prevent cancer.[67, 68] From a hallmarks-of-aging perspective, vitamin D can aid in maintaining telomere length and in intercellular communication.[69, 70]

Cats do not make their own vitamin D from sunlight like we humans do, and in my experience, many cats are deficient (see more about this in Chapter 2). Since both age-related sarcopenia and cancer are widespread among cats, vitamin D is absolutely something that should be monitored and, when needed, supplemented. The amount of vitamin D to supplement is dependent on blood levels, so get your kitty tested. It is possible to overdose vitamin D, so blindly supplementing is not recommended, although the amount of vitamin D found in a multivitamin for cats is fine. Symptoms of vitamin D overdose include a buildup of calcium that may lead to kidney damage and/or the formation of calcium-based kidney or bladder stones. Vitamin D is a fat-soluble vitamin, so it should be given with food.

Vitamin E

Vitamin E is an antioxidant and anti-inflammatory, and may lower the risk of cancer.[71] Vitamin E also reduces mitochondrial dysfunction, enhances cognitive performance, and can improve signs of arthritis in dogs, so it is likely to have the same effect in kitties.[72, 73, 74]

Natural sources of vitamin E include nuts, seeds, and leafy greens. Vitamin E can also be given within a multivitamin made for cats. If using a multivitamin for humans, check with your veterinarian or a veterinary nutritionist for a specific dose. As a standalone supplement, vitamin E, generally in the form of alpha-tocopherol, can be dosed in the range of 50 to 100 IU. Vitamin E is fat-soluble, so it should be given with food.

Vitamin K

There are two forms of Vitamin K: K_1, which plays a role in blood clotting, and K_2, which impacts calcium transport and deposition in the bones.[75] Both K vitamins affect aging and longevity by limiting the senescent cell burden through promoting apoptosis, modulating inflammation and oxidative stress, and preventing mitochondrial dysfunction.[76] They also have anticancer properties and, along with vitamin D, help regulate calcium within the body.[77]

There is generally no need to supplement vitamin K_1, assuming your cat is eating a properly balanced diet. But if you are supplementing vitamin D, you should also add vitamin K_2, and there are supplements that contain both. K_2 comes in two forms: MK-4 and MK-7. MK-7 is the preferred choice, at a dose of 10 to 20 micrograms per day along with vitamin D. As vitamins K and D are both fat-soluble, administer with food for best absorption. If using a multivitamin for cats, give the recommended dose. If using a multivitamin for humans, consult your veterinarian or a veterinary nutritionist for the right dose.

Zinc

Zinc is a micronutrient that has wide-ranging effects with regard to longevity. Zinc promotes immune system function, limits oxidative stress and inflammaging, and prevents mitochondrial dysfunction.[78, 79] For supplementation, use a dose of 5 to 10 milligrams per day.

SUPPLEMENTATION STRATEGIES

Longevity is, by definition, a long-term practice. Giving everything at once is both unnecessary and, frankly, impossible with just about any cat I have ever met. Rotating through and alternating supplements is an excellent way to obtain the biggest benefits while not having to give too much at any one time. In addition, certain supplements are good for the long term, while others should be on a periodic rotation. The ideal scenario is to add your cat's supplements to their food whenever possible, because giving long-term supplements orally is often not sustainable.

Long Term

First on the shortlist for long-term supplementation are probiotics. The bottom line here is that gut health is the cornerstone of immune system health and whole-body health. There may be benefits in periodically rotating through different probiotics to give your cat's body a variety of bacteria, but having them on some kind of probiotic for the long term is recommended.

Omega-3 fatty acids, like EPA, DHA, and ALA, are also great long-term additions to support longevity. I highly recommend supplementing EPA and DHA in the form of fish oil. When it becomes available, test your cat's omega-3 levels once or twice yearly to ensure appropriate supplementation. When it comes to ALA, there is frequently a good amount in food, so while it is still excellent to supplement, it is not an absolute necessity.

Vitamin D is another great long-term supplement if your cat is deficient. Many, but not all, cats I test are low in vitamin D. The amount of vitamin D found in an appropriate multivitamin for animals is fine for all cats, although it may not be enough. Vitamin D testing is a great way both to quantify the need for supplementation and to confirm that the amount you are supplementing is appropriate.

Periodic

Pretty much everything else on the list can be used on a periodic-rotation basis—and you don't need to use everything. In my experience, most pet owners have a maximum number of supplements they can give before it starts becoming a pain in the you-know-what. I certainly do have clients who are giving their pets 20 supplements daily, but I'm not expecting you to do this, unless you want to and have a remarkably compliant kitty.

From a strategic perspective, try to determine what is realistically possible with your cat and pick two or three off the list that have complementary actions against the hallmarks of aging. In other words, try to check as many of the nine original boxes as you can with those two or three supplements. If you can only "get away with" one at a time, that is just fine. Alternatively, there are combination supplements out there that have several of the listed nutrients, so you may be able to check a lot of boxes with just one product.

Either way, give your chosen supplements for a period of time, such as every three months, and then shift to different ones. By adjusting supplements four times per year, you will provide your cat with a wide range of benefits, and it won't become overwhelming.

* * *

There are other longevity-promoting treatments that fall outside the supplement category, such as peptides, pharmaceuticals, and interventional therapies that can be integrated into your cat's longevity plan. We will discuss these in the next chapter. The ultimate goal is to compile everything into a sustainable, comprehensive strategy.

SUPPLEMENTS AND THE HALLMARKS OF AGING

	Genomic Instability	Telomere Attrition	Epigenetic Alterations	Loss of Proteostasis
Ashwagandha		■		
Berberine				
Carotenoids	■			
CoQ10	■			
Curcumin	■			
EGCG			■	
Essential Fatty Acids	■	■		
Fisetin				
Magnesium				
Melatonin				
Mushrooms				
N-Acetylcysteine	■			
NMN				
Oleuropein Aglycone				■
Plasmalogens				
Probiotics				
Pterostilbene				■
Pycnogenol				
Quercetin				■
Resveratrol			■	■
Selenium	■			
Serine				■
Spermidine				■
Suforaphane	■			■
Vitamin A	■			
Vitamin B			■	
Vitamin C	■	■		
Vitamin D		■		
Vitamin E				
Vitamin K				
Zinc				

Deregulated Nutrient Sensing	Mitochondrial Dysfunction	Cellular Senescence	Stem Cell Exhaustion	Altered Intercellular Communication

PART IV

THE FUTURE IS HERE

CHAPTER 7

REGENERATIVE THERAPIES AND MEDICINE

The hallmarks of aging provide us with a framework within which we can discover and utilize tools to slow, and possibly even stop, what most people consider inevitable. Understanding the mechanics of what causes our cats to age and how we can intervene in these processes through nutrition, lifestyle, and supplementation charts a course toward health and longevity for our cats. But that is only the beginning. . . .

We are in a unique position at this moment in time. We are the first generation who has the ability to truly understand and begin to slow the aging process, and the science of longevity is rapidly expanding. New drug therapies are being utilized to slow aging, and some older ones are being repurposed to do the same. Technology is also being leveraged to slow the aging process, and treatments for difficult chronic conditions are within our grasp. In this context, longevity medicine is about more than merely addressing the hallmarks of aging—it is about treating medical conditions that will affect both quality and quantity of life.

In this chapter, we will explore longevity therapies and medications that are currently available in the veterinary space and those that will be a part of it in the very near future. As we examine these more advanced longevity options for cats, it is important to highlight that there is essentially no feline-specific clinical research for these methods. As it turns out, all the therapies to follow are used on humans with little clinical research as well. Unlike last chapter's discussion of supplements, everything to follow should be done under a veterinarian's supervision. As you are about to see, things are getting very exciting!

OXYGEN THERAPIES

We all know oxygen is important. When we breathe in, oxygen flows into our body, and when we breathe out, carbon dioxide flows out, in the process called respiration. But do you know what happens from there? There is another, much deeper form of respiration called *cellular respiration.*

Earlier, we discussed mitochondrial dysfunction as a hallmark of aging. Mitochondria are the structures within cells that generate the energy that allows every cell in the body to conduct its business. Cellular respiration is a chemical process within mitochondria that generates energy in the form of a molecule called adenosine triphosphate (ATP), and oxygen is required. Without it, the mitochondria's ability to generate ATP is severely limited, and if cells are starved of oxygen long enough, the lack of ATP will cause them to die—or worse.

Decreased oxygenation of tissues is known as *hypoxia.* Hypoxia occurs when the body is not able to deliver oxygen to an area. Systemically, this can be caused by an inability to absorb or circulate oxygen as a result of heart, lung, or circulation disease, as well as anemia (not enough red blood cells). On a more local level, hypoxia occurs after an interruption of circulation due to injury, swelling or inflammation, or occlusion of a blood vessel (embolus). Regardless of the cause, a lack of oxygen dramatically slows tissue healing and regeneration and is associated with cellular aging and potentially the development of cancer.[1, 2, 3]

If a lack of oxygen causes all this trouble, why not just let our cats breathe oxygen and help them feel and be better? Unfortunately, it's not quite that easy. You see, the red blood cells that carry oxygen are generally 95 percent saturated with oxygen when your cat is breathing regular room air. You can bump that up to 100 percent by having them breathe pure oxygen, but that extra 5 percent really isn't making that much difference. And if the hypoxia is localized in an area with compromised circulation, the body's red blood cells are not able to deliver the oxygen. There are, however, methods to dramatically increase oxygen levels.

Hyperbaric Oxygen Therapy

Hyperbaric oxygen therapy (HBOT) is a procedure in which a patient is placed in a chamber that pressurizes while they—in this case, your cat—breathe 100 percent oxygen. The technology itself goes back as far as the 1600s and was used for a variety of medical issues, albeit with little scientific basis.[4] In more modern times, HBOT was used starting in the 1940s for decompression sickness in deep-sea divers, and later for carbon monoxide poisoning. Since it is unlikely your cat is scuba diving, and carbon monoxide poisoning these days is quite rare even in people, we want to focus on the newer applications of HBOT.

HBOT works through the presence of high concentrations of oxygen and a pressure gradient. Effectively what is happening is that breathing oxygen at high pressure forces it into the bloodstream. The reason HBOT works is because oxygen under pressure dissolves into the plasma (the liquid portion of blood), resulting in the blood being able to carry up to 20 times more oxygen than if the patient were breathing room air alone. As oxygen-saturated blood flows through the body, the oxygen will naturally diffuse into areas where concentrations are lower. Because the oxygen is dissolved in the plasma, it doesn't require a red blood cell to carry it to the site where it is needed. This means that in areas where circulation is compromised due to injury, swelling, and so forth, oxygen can passively diffuse into hypoxic tissues, just like a sponge absorbs water without any assistance. The presence of more oxygen fuels mitochondria, which then generates ATP and allows cells to function and tissues to heal. There is a lot of physics behind the scenes making this all happen, but you get the picture.

In human medicine, HBOT is commonly used in the treatment of nonhealing wounds, such as diabetic ulcers, burns caused by radiation therapy, and deep-seated infections such as osteomyelitis (bone infection).[5, 6] It also has therapeutic effects on certain types of cancers.[7] While we don't see diabetic ulcers in cats, we certainly do encounter nonhealing wounds of other kinds, as well as radiation burns and difficult-to-treat infections. There are many other therapeutic uses for HBOT in cats, including organ disease such as pancreatitis or hepatitis, spinal cord compression from a ruptured disc or other trauma, head injury and stroke, and so on. On more than one occasion, I have had a veterinarian refer a patient with an injury or infection that literally threatens both life and limb. We have saved patients from amputations and unquestionably saved lives with HBOT when allopathic medical options have failed.

Many people have a concern that using HBOT for the treatment of cancer may "feed" oxygen to cancer cells and make them grow faster. After all, oxygen is a key factor in the production of ATP. Fortunately, this turns out not to be the case. Cancer cells tend to have alterations in their mitochondria that change the way they produce ATP, and in short, they prefer a low-oxygen environment with limited blood supply. Within this hypoxic environment, cancer cells are able to generate energy while shielding themselves from the immune system and anticancer therapeutics such as chemotherapy, herbal therapy, and so forth. Hyperbaric oxygen increases tissue oxygenation throughout the entire body, including tumors. The increase in oxygen concentration within and around cancer can induce apoptosis (programmed cell death) and slow the proliferation of the cancer cells.[8, 9]

HBOT also has specific effects on the hallmarks of aging, including increasing telomere length, decreasing senescent cell burden,[10] and increasing stem cell proliferation, which leads to an increase in the ability of the body to heal wounds and other areas of inflammation and tissue damage.[11] Genomic instability, yet another hallmark, ultimately leads to changes in gene expression and the transcriptome, or the spectrum and function of proteins created from the DNA template. In humans, HBOT has been proven to alter the transcriptome of elderly patients to a younger state.[12] Lastly, HBOT improves cognitive function in older adults, which may be beneficial for cats, as we do see cognitive decline in some as they age.[13]

One final note regarding HBOT: Therapy requires multiple treatments. Depending on the condition, HBOT therapy for a person might include anywhere from 10 to

50 treatments or more. In veterinary medicine, we aren't always able to do this many treatments, as it would require a significant investment of time and finances on the part of the owner. That said, even fewer treatments than might be conducted in a human with a similar condition can still be effective. HBOT does not enjoy widespread use in veterinary (or human) medicine, although an increasing number of holistic and integrative veterinarians are bringing this technology into their offices. Depending on the indication, HBOT is also covered by some pet insurance policies.

OZONE

You may be familiar with ozone, although probably not in the context of health and longevity. Strictly speaking, ozone is a different molecular form of oxygen. Normally, two oxygen atoms bind together to form a stable molecule known as O_2. This is the form of oxygen you are breathing in the air right now. Ozone is an unstable grouping of three oxygen atoms, or O_3. Environmentally, ozone naturally occurs in the upper atmosphere (the ozone layer) as a result of O_2 being exposed to ultraviolet (UV) light, which converts it to O_3. The ozone layer protects us from many of the harmful effects of UV radiation from the sun. Down here on the surface, ozone is an air pollutant that can cause respiratory irritation.

Given that being directly exposed to ozone gas leads to respiratory irritation, you might ask how ozone can promote health and longevity. Ozone can be administered in multiple ways that do not involve breathing it in. Ozone gas can be given rectally to be absorbed into the bloodstream, subcutaneously (under the skin), or intravenously in the form of ozonated saline that is sometimes mixed with the patient's blood. Ozone gas can also be used topically in a process called limb bagging or through the application of ozonated oil. Lastly, ozone can be used as an oral rinse or consumed in the form of ozonated water.

Ozone works within the body to promote health in more than one way. One of the primary ways is through hormetic stress. This is a process by which an organism experiences a degree of environmental stress that makes the body stronger. Let's say you go to the gym and lift weights and are sore the next day. If I biopsied your sore muscle, what we would see is widespread damage to muscle fibers on a microscopic level. This microtrauma (stress) ultimately stimulates the body to create more and stronger muscle. Hormetic stress to the immune system works very similarly.

I mentioned that the ozone molecule is unstable; it wants to go back to being O_2.[14, 15, 16, 17, 18] The chemical process of ozone breaking apart leads to the formation of hydrogen peroxide and many other compounds in the body that cause oxidation. Antioxidants are compounds that protect the body from the oxidative damage that occurs as a result of normal physiological processes as well as external factors. The "micro-oxidation" caused by the ozone stimulates the body to increase production of natural antioxidants and a variety of other compounds involved with immune system function.[19, 20, 21] So, the hormetic stress caused by ozone leads to a better-functioning immune system.

Because ozone increases the amount of oxygen in tissues, it also supports mitochondrial function and the generation of ATP. Ozone is intensely antimicrobial as well—so much so that it is sometimes used to sterilize surgical instruments—and kills bacteria on contact, making it particularly useful for topical applications to treat infected wounds. In addition, ozone is being researched for its effects on preventing neurodegeneration and cognitive decline in older people. As we previously discussed regarding HBOT, cancer cells thrive in a hypoxic environment, and exposing them to ozone has been shown to induce apoptosis (programmed cell death) through a variety of mechanisms. Additionally, ozone can improve the efficacy of chemotherapy and radiation therapy in cancer patients.[22, 23] Increases in tissue oxygenation and antioxidant production, and subsequent reduction in inflammation, are vital components of keeping cells healthy and promoting longevity.

Like HBOT, ozone therapy is not something every veterinary office offers, but veterinarians offering ozone are out there. There are many protocols for the use of ozone, and a veterinarian experienced with ozone therapy will be able to guide you to the ones that will best fit your cat's needs.

REGENERATIVE MEDICINE

A common theme in longevity medicine is finding ways to utilize the body's natural systems to slow the aging process. One of the most direct ways to do this is by taking healing factors from the body—such as cells, proteins, hormones, and so on that the body naturally produces to facilitate healing—and using them to treat injury or damaged tissues. Using cells or other factors that come from a patient's own body as medicine is called *autologous therapy*. This is most commonly conducted through the use of platelet-rich plasma (PRP) and/or stem cell therapy, and in addition to its therapeutic benefits, it has essentially no risk of side effects, since your cat is receiving something that came from their body. There are also regenerative options that utilize cells or other factors from a healthy animal to benefit one with an issue. Let's explore a few of these options.

Platelet-Rich Plasma

Blood is a combination of solids and liquids. The solids—red blood cells, white blood cells, and platelets—are suspended in liquid (plasma). When the red and white cells are removed from the blood, what remains are platelets suspended in plasma, or platelet-rich plasma (PRP). Platelets play a critical role in blood clotting. If your cat is injured, they help stop the bleeding. The platelets don't stop there, however. They also play a large part in wound healing through promoting the formation of new blood vessels and tissue repair. This is the activity we are looking for by using PRP.

PRP is most commonly used to treat injuries and/or arthritis via injection into the affected site. In human athletes, PRP is commonly a part of the therapy for torn tendons and muscles, rotator-cuff (shoulder) injuries, and so forth. Human medicine is also finding more applications for PRP, including cosmetic procedures and improving the success of hair transplants. While we aren't going to be discussing face-lifts and new hair for your cat, this gives you an idea of the widespread potential uses of something that is already in everyone's body.

In veterinary medicine, the most common use of PRP is to improve functionality and pain in cats with arthritis. That said, it has also been shown to be effective for the treatment of a variety of other conditions, including tendon injuries, cartilage damage, and bone fractures. Just like in humans, we inject the PRP into and around the site of the injury to help stimulate healing. It can also be applied topically to treat burns, wounds, and even corneal (surface of the eye) injuries.[24] PRP is an accepted form of treatment in veterinary medicine, although not too many general practitioners offer it. More commonly, PRP is administered by a veterinary specialist, such as a surgeon. Even so, it's not a complicated procedure in most cases, and pet insurance will often cover it.

From a longevity perspective, PRP's uses are largely related to promoting healing and limiting pain. While there are likely specific effects on one or more of the hallmarks of aging, they haven't been fully evaluated. Setting aside the hallmarks, aging is ultimately a function of the body no longer being able to repair itself. By intervening with a healing therapy such as PRP to improve mobility and function, we are, by definition, promoting longevity.

Stem Cell Therapy

No doubt you have heard of stem cell therapy. It has been in the news for years both for its potential as an effective therapy and also due to some controversy regarding where the stem cells are harvested. Within the context of veterinary medicine and autologous therapy, all the stem cells we are talking about come from your own cat.

Stem cells are one of the most powerful cell types in the body. Almost all cells in the body have a specific job to do. Heart cells make up the heart muscle, kidney cells make up the kidneys, skin cells make up the skin, and so on. As a rule, these cells will do their job within their particular area of expertise until they are too old to function, and then they are recycled by the body.

When the body needs to replace cells, it has two options. Some cells, such as those within the skin, liver, and GI tract, are able to divide and create new cells to fill the gap. Other tissues, like the heart and kidneys, are not as adept at doing this. When local tissue regeneration is not possible due to either the cell type or extent of damage, stem cells come into play.

Think of stem cells like a young child with her whole life ahead of her. In that moment, she has the potential to become anything. As she gets older and makes choices in her life, the possibilities narrow. At some point (hopefully), she will decide what she wants to do; focus her abilities on that; and emerge as a doctor, lawyer, musician, artist, or anything else. Stem cells are created as a blank slate to provide the body with a source of material to repair and replace tissues throughout the body. To be clear, there are many types of stem cells, and their abilities differ. For the purposes of this discussion, we are focusing on mesenchymal stem cells (MSCs), as these are the ones currently in use in veterinary medicine.

The term *mesenchymal* refers to connective tissue within the body. Connective tissue makes up a broad swath of body structures, including bone, cartilage, blood-vessel walls, fat, and so forth. MSCs are stem cells that can transform into any of these tissues. To use the previous analogy, our little girl has decided she likes science and is focusing her efforts on this. She could become a doctor, a pharmacist, a researcher, or even an astronaut, but most likely law school or a career as a professional musician is off the table. MSCs have a lot of options, but they do not have the ability to transform into non-mesenchymal tissues such as heart cells or brain cells.

In practical terms, MSCs are mostly used for orthopedic conditions, such as arthritis and tendon injuries. The process begins with harvesting the stem cells, which can be achieved from bone marrow or fat. In veterinary medicine, we mostly collect from fat, as it is more easily accessible. The cat is briefly anesthetized, and your veterinarian makes a small incision over their abdomen to collect fat—even thin cats will have some fatty tissue around their liver. The collection process is quick, as is recovery. The harvested fat is then processed to extract the stem cells. Usually this is done by overnighting the tissue to a lab. The lab extracts the cells, places them in syringes, and overnights them back. Any extra cells are banked for future use.

The process of administering MSCs is usually via a local injection at the site of the problem. Your veterinarian may, for example, inject your cat's arthritic hip or knee. If your cat has a soft-tissue injury such a tendon tear, they would inject the tendon directly. Usually these injections require sedation, but overall the process is quick and relatively painless. Positive effects can be seen from within days to months, depending on the individual and their condition, and sometimes are dramatic—cats are suddenly running around and feeling better than they have in a long time. All in all, the entire process from harvest to administration takes about 48 hours and can be repeated as necessary. For repeat injections, surgical collection is not required, as the laboratory can use the banked cells collected the first time.

Sometimes MSCs are injected intravenously for other issues such as kidney disease. This sounds like a great idea to address deeper issues, like failing organs and neurologic conditions, but there is a hitch. When we were discussing hyperbaric oxygen, I mentioned how oxygen is "picked up" by the blood in the lungs and then distributed to the entire body. The concern with MSCs is the other side of the circulatory pathway. After the blood delivers oxygen and nutrients to the body, it returns to the heart, where it is pumped back into the lungs. Blood that enters the lungs passes through smaller and smaller blood vessels, down to the level of microcapillaries—tiny vessels that facilitate the exchange of oxygen and carbon dioxide within the lungs. Microcapillaries are 8 to 10 micrometers (microns) in diameter (a micron is 0.001 millimeter). That's barely enough room for red blood cells to fit through, and the larger white blood cells frequently have to squeeze through by changing their shape. MSCs are about 20 micrometers in diameter.

In short, they don't fit, and they get "hung up" in the microcapillaries in the same way peas stay in a strainer after the water has drained. Research shows that few, if any, MSCs can be found anywhere in the body other than the lungs following intravenous infusion.[25, 26] To be clear, this process is not harmful to the lungs, and there is evidence to suggest using MSCs in this way is an effective way to treat diseases of the lung such as emphysema and pulmonary hypertension, among others. It's just not useful to treat other areas of the body.[27, 28]

Very Small Embryonic-Like Stem Cells

A lot of research is being funneled into stem cell therapy for obvious reasons. The prospect of being able to regenerate damaged or diseased areas of the body is highly appealing. Beyond MSCs, whose advantages and limitations we just discussed, other types of stem cells are under study.

Embryonic stem cells are taken from fetal tissue and have the ability to transform into any cell type in the body. They can also be collected from umbilical-cord blood from newborns. Both have the potential to help aging cats, but as a practical matter neither of these are viable options given the ethical considerations of collecting fetal tissue from pregnant cats and the fact that few kittens are born in a hospital setting, making umbilical-cord-blood storage impossible.

Induced pluripotent stem cells have similar properties to embryonic stem cells, but they are created from "regular" cells. Essentially, cells from the body can be treated with specific compounds known as Yamanaka factors and can be transformed backward into a cell very similar to an embryonic stem cell. The researcher who discovered this process,

Shinya Yamanaka, received a Nobel Prize in 2012 for this work. There is a lot of potential here, but these stem cells are not ready for prime time, as they appear to be prone to causing benign tumors known as teratomas.

There is another type of stem cell you have likely never heard of. In fact, most veterinarians and physicians have never heard of them. *Very small embryonic-like stem cells* (VSELs) were originally described in the scientific literature as early as 2008, but their function—and in some circles, their very existence—was questioned.[29] These cells are present in tissues throughout the body and circulate through the blood. They appear to be the body's version of reserve embryonic stem cells. In other words, they are able to transform into any tissue type in the body, as opposed to more specialized stem cells like MSCs. As the name would imply, VSELs are small, around 5 micrometers. This, of course, means they can live in circulating blood and pass through the lungs, unlike the much larger MSCs. Although research is ongoing, it is safe to say VSELs are used by the body to repair tissues in the event of injury or other damage.[30]

Another fascinating characteristic of VSELs is that they don't appear to age.[31] Other stem cells tend to be less effective when they are collected from an older patient. (Remember, stem cell exhaustion is one of the hallmarks of aging.) The trouble is, more often than not, the patient who needs stem cell therapy is middle-aged or older. VSELs are essentially dormant until they are needed, and this metabolic inactivity means they don't age like other cells. Thus, the VSELs of a 15-year-old cat are, at least in theory, as potent as the day the cat was born.

I suspect you are starting to see what is so interesting about VSELs. It appears they have the benefits of embryonic stem cells, do not necessitate collection under difficult or controversial circumstances, and are "good as new," regardless of the age of the patient. Until recently, however, all of this was purely a laboratory exercise and not used in clinical practice as a result of the medical community being slow to realize the potential of these newly discovered cells. Thankfully, that is changing.

A physician and researcher in Southern California named Todd Ovokaitys has discovered some other interesting properties of VSELs and found a way to utilize them to treat patients.[32, 33] Dr. Todd, as he is called, was doing VSEL research and had the cells in a dish. He used a laser to project a beam through the center of the dish for three minutes and something pretty surprising happened. The dormant VSELs began to rapidly reproduce, and instead of being distributed throughout the dish, the cells moved into a line along the axis of where the laser had been. To make a very complex story short, the laser "woke up" the VSELs and changed the expression of proteins on the surface of the cells, making them adhere to one another. The cells effectively became "sticky."

This discovery led Dr. Todd to develop a procedure to extract and separate VSELs from a blood sample in much the same way we discussed earlier for PRP. In fact, this procedure is really a combination of PRP and stem cell therapy. The PRP, which contains VSELs, is exposed to a very specific type of laser (also designed by Dr. Todd) that wakes up the VSELs. At this point, the VSEL/PRP solution can either be administered directly into an affected area, such as an arthritic joint, or be given intravenously, since the VSELs are so small that they pass through the lungs with no problem.

Once the cells are administered, the same laser that was used to wake up the VSELs is directed at the body part(s) being targeted for the treatment. As the cells move through the circulation and past the area being lasered, they become "sticky" and tend to stay in that area. The goal is for the VSELs to be concentrated in the area of the body being treated. This is of particular value for internal organs or the brain and spinal cord, as these areas are difficult to inject directly.

VSEL therapy holds a lot of promise, and there are reports from humans being treated that are nothing short of miraculous, such as people's heart function improving so much they are no longer in need of a transplant, along with reports of improved vision, joint function, cognition, and so forth. While studies have evaluated the use of VSELs for the treatment of conditions such as heart disease and for the rejuvenation of tissues, there are currently no published clinical trials on the procedure developed by Dr. Todd, although that is likely to change.[34, 35]

On the veterinary side, I am extremely fortunate to be the first veterinarian to use Dr. Todd's procedure on patients, and we are seeing similar results. To my knowledge, the first cat to receive VSEL therapy is my own kitty, Frieda. I don't know exactly how old Frieda is, as she came to my family when our neighbors moved away and left her behind. That sounds horrible—and it is—but . . . in the end, we lost a bad neighbor and gained a great kitty, so it all worked out. Anyway, Frieda was a young adult then, and my daughter, Abbey, was about four months old. Abbey is now a college freshman and Frieda is still bopping around my house, so we are assuming she is somewhere north of 20 years old.

As soon as I was able to provide VSEL therapy in my office, Frieda was high on the list of "volunteers." For a cat of her age, she is in pretty good shape, but she is definitely arthritic and her hind end doesn't work great. She clearly has some trouble getting around. She received one treatment, and within a few days, there was a demonstrable improvement in her mobility and energy level. The VSELs certainly did not turn Frieda into a kitten again, but there is no question her quality of life improved. Frieda is a member of my family, and to see her feeling and moving better was incredibly gratifying and has made me even more excited to be able to offer this cutting-edge therapy for my feline patients.

While VSEL therapy is not currently a widely available option for veterinary or human patients, it will be found in more and more clinics over time. Most patients do require more than one treatment, and the best results appear to be when the treatment is repeated at regular intervals, somewhere between one to four times yearly.

MICROBIOME RESTORATIVE THERAPY

Microbiome restorative therapy (MBRT) is the more formal name for fecal transplants (I'm guessing you probably just made an unpleasant sound). A fecal transplant is exactly what it sounds like: a stool sample (feces) from a healthy cat is put into a cat that has medical issues, such as chronic gastrointestinal disease, allergies, or other conditions associated with an imbalance of the immune system.

As I mentioned in the discussion of probiotics, 70 percent of the immune system lives in the gut, meaning imbalances of gut flora can have a broad impact on overall health, far beyond signs of GI distress. Gut flora has, in fact, been linked to allergies, cognitive dysfunction, and Parkinson's disease in humans.[36, 37, 38] Probiotics can help restore healthy gut flora, but there are limits to what they can do. Probiotics work by creating an environment in the gut that is friendly to beneficial bacteria and does not support the growth of harmful ones. There is a common misconception that probiotics are recolonizing the gut with new bacteria, but this is not the case. Not long after you stop giving them, the bacterial strains in the probiotic are gone. This is why you need to keep giving them long term.

MBRT works differently, because it can help restore healthy gut flora for the long term. Cats may have unhealthy flora for a variety of reasons, including poor diet, antibiotic use, and chemotherapy.[39, 40] Sometimes probiotics are enough to restore the balance, but in more severe cases, MBRT is required. More specifically pertaining to aging and longevity, fecal transplantations from young mice into older mice have been shown to reverse hallmarks of aging in the gut, eyes, and brain.[41]

In veterinary medicine, fecal transplantation was pioneered by a veterinarian named Margo Roman in Massachusetts, and she has been using MBRT alongside ozone therapy for years, often with dramatically positive results. She also coined the term *microbiome restorative therapy.* Fecal material from prescreened healthy cats is administered rectally, and sometimes orally, in the form of frozen fecal material in capsules. The procedure frequently is repeated several times over a period of months to achieve the greatest effects.

One of the earliest examples of successful regenerative therapy I witnessed firsthand was in a cat that belonged to a veterinary technician working in my office. Lester was an adorable kitty with a chronic diarrhea problem. He had been through all the standard diagnostic tests. The diagnosis from the internal medicine specialist was inflammatory bowel disease (IBD), and it wasn't responding to conventional treatments. This was years ago and I was only just beginning to explore regenerative medicine at the time, so when the internal medicine specialist suggested a fecal transplant, I was intrigued. The doctor performed a fecal transplant procedure and then another one a few weeks later. I'd never seen something like this done before, so you can imagine my surprise when Lester started having normal stools for the first time in more than a year! Over time, he was taken off all his medications, and he never needed treatment for IBD again. There are moments in everyone's life, both personal and professional, that are so impactful, they change your perception of "how things are." For me, this was one of those moments.

Other protocols utilize freeze-dried fecal transplant material given orally in capsules, although I have not seen dramatically positive results with this method. This probably goes without saying, *but don't try this at home*. Work with a veterinarian with experience in fecal transplantation.

PLASMA REPLACEMENT

As we have previously discussed, plasma is the liquid fraction of blood. You can also think of it as blood minus the red and white blood cells. Platelets may or may not be present, depending on if we are discussing pure plasma or platelet-rich plasma. Regardless, plasma isn't merely the liquid blood cells are suspended in. It has a significant purpose, including maintaining osmotic pressure, or the balance of fluid inside and outside of cells. It also serves as a carrier for vital blood proteins, sugar, fats, and cell-signaling compounds like hormones.

Scientists have been evaluating the effects of taking blood from one animal and putting it into another for well over 100 years. These studies have led to advancements in multiple fields of medicine, including immunology, oncology, and endocrinology. There is also an interesting facet of this type of study pertaining to longevity.

Initial research into this field is a little weird. In a process called heterochronic parabiosis, researchers took an old mouse and a young mouse and literally sewed them together so they shared a circulatory system.[42] Not necessarily the most humane research trial, but most of these things occurred 50 or more years ago. Setting aside the creepy factor, something really interesting came of these studies. When the mice of different ages were surgically connected, the young mouse got "older" and the old mouse got "younger," raising the question of how the components of blood are related to aging.

If old blood promotes "oldness" and young blood promotes "youngness," what factors are at play? If putting young blood into an older animal has a positive effect, is it because there are components in young blood that promote youth, or is it that we are diluting out factors in old blood that promote aging? Conversely, if old blood will age a young animal, are we infusing aging factors into young blood, or are we diluting out the youthful factors and making them less abundant? It would appear the answer is yes across the board. Since no one in their right mind is advocating cats being surgically connected or using young cats as blood donors to keep older ones healthy, is there a less vampirish way to leverage this very interesting information? It turns out there are several.

The least complicated solution is therapeutic plasma exchange. You are probably familiar with donating plasma, and perhaps you have even done it. You donate blood, and then the plasma is removed and your red blood cells are returned through an IV infusion. From a longevity perspective, the same process can be done in order to dilute out the "old" factors in blood.[43, 44] It's kind of like doing a half water change in a fish tank. The water becomes much cleaner, even though you didn't replace all of it. The challenge here from a cat-treatment perspective is that there aren't really facilities that will do this. Plasma is extracted at facilities that supply veterinarians with blood-transfusion products, but this is not the kind of equipment any veterinarian has in their office.

Another approach is to add youthful factors to an older cat's body through a plasma transfusion from a younger cat. The issue here, of course, is that using the blood of young animals as a longevity therapeutic for older animals is unethical, pure and simple. There is simply no way to make this okay. That said, there are groups currently working on creating synthetic products that mimic "young plasma." In the future, it may be possible to purchase a bag of synthetic "young cat plasma" and infuse it into older animals in order to promote longevity.

Perhaps the most complicated way to "clean up" an older person's blood is through plasmapheresis. In this process, a patient is hooked up to a machine that extracts blood, cleans the plasma, and then returns it. This process is similar to dialysis for kidney patients. As you might imagine, plasmapheresis is very expensive and, as such, not currently available for veterinary patients.

Plasma replacement shows a lot of promise, but we are still a ways away from this being a practical component of longevity therapy for your cat. It is definitely something to keep an eye out for in the future.

DRUGS

Considering how much science is involved with the quest for longevity, you might think there would be more pharmaceuticals available. Undoubtedly, drugs will be developed specifically for the purposes of longevity medicine, but for now this list is relatively short. That said, the two drugs discussed below are powerful options for our quest to help our cats live longer and better.

Rapamycin

Rapamycin is a drug with a fascinating history. It was originally discovered as a compound produced by a particular bacteria present on Easter Island. The name, in fact, comes from the traditional one for Easter Island, Rapa Nui. Rapamycin has conventionally been used in organ-transplant patients to help prevent tissue rejection, and in recent years it has received a lot of attention for its longevity-promoting properties.

In Chapter 2, we discussed the mammalian target of rapamycin, or mTOR. This pathway helps regulate nutrient sensing in the body and specifically promotes tissue growth, which can be good or bad, depending on what tissue is growing. Rapamycin inhibits mTOR and thus slows tissue growth. At appropriate doses, rapamycin has anticancer properties; supports cardiovascular, immune system, and cognitive function; and helps animals live longer.[45, 46] In short, rapamycin is one of the most interesting and promising pharmaceutical interventions currently available in the longevity space.

Rapamycin dosing has to be done very carefully, however, and it is not something to be given every day. You may remember we previously discussed the balance between mTOR and AMPK, which modulates the body's ability to both create and break down cells. Both are critical to health and longevity, and everything has to be in balance. Many longevity-focused physicians recommend cycling rapamycin use in humans once weekly, and an ongoing research trial known as the Dog Longevity Project is evaluating the effects of rapamycin on dogs.[47] While they have not evaluated cats at this time, there is every reason to believe the effects will be similar. There are ongoing studies looking at the use of rapamycin to treat hypertrophic cardiomyopathy, a common form of heart disease in cats. I am intentionally not providing dosing information on rapamycin, because this drug can be dangerous if used improperly. Please only try this under direct veterinary supervision.

Dasatinib

Dasatinib is a chemotherapy drug used to treat leukemia in people. Pharmacologically speaking, it is known as a tyrosine kinase inhibitor. Tyrosine kinase is a protein that signals cells to divide, and in some cancer cells, the protein is abnormal and leads to uncontrolled cellular division. Dasatinib blocks the action of tyrosine kinase and thus can slow the progression of cancers like leukemia in humans.

Dasatinib, in conjunction with quercetin (see Chapter 6), is also a potent senolytic, meaning it has the ability to kill senescent cells in the body. As you recall, senescent cells no longer function as healthy cells, and they also resist being eliminated by the body. Cellular senescence is one of the hallmarks of aging, because these cells frequently secrete chemical compounds that promote the formation of more senescent cells, which decreases the body's ability to function optimally (aging) and, in the process, potentially promotes the formation of cancer.[48, 49] Senolytics have also been demonstrated to increase physical function and improve life span in research animals through a variety of cellular pathways. The combination of dasatinib and quercetin has shown impressive senolytic effect and is one of the more promising approaches to address this particular hallmark of aging.[50, 51, 52] To my knowledge, dasatinib has not been used in cats for longevity purposes . . . yet.

Senolytic cells take time to accumulate, which means senolytics can be used intermittently in a "hit and run" approach.[53] The goal is to reduce your cat's senescent cell burden and then stop the treatment. Potent senolytics like dasatinib do not, and should not, be given on a regular basis. Remember, this is not a supplement with a wide range of safety. Dasatinib can cause side effects, such as heart and lung damage, if used long term or at improper doses. In addition, it's important to note that dasatinib has been studied in dogs as a chemotherapy agent but not as a senolytic. There is every reason to presume combining it with quercetin could be an effective antiaging therapy for dogs and cats, but more research is required for us to know for sure.

PEPTIDE THERAPY

Amino acids are strung together based on instructions from DNA to form peptides, polypeptides, and ultimately proteins. Peptides and polypeptides are utilized by the body for a variety of reasons, including functioning as hormones, growth factors, neurotransmitters, and other cell-signaling compounds that provide instructions to the body.

Peptide therapy is the use of peptides either orally or via injection to promote certain processes in the body that help treat medical conditions and promote longevity. They are frequently "stacked," meaning a patient will receive more than one peptide in a given treatment cycle. Treatment cycles usually are around two months, although this can vary depending on the individual and goals of therapy. There is a long list of peptides being used for this purpose.

Currently, peptide therapy is not being widely offered in the veterinary space, although this is likely to change, so it is important for you, as a longevity-focused cat parent, to be aware of it. The following are a few of the most commonly used peptides in humans that are also promising for cats.

BPC 157

Body protection compound 157 (BPC 157) is a peptide that is naturally produced in the stomach.[54, 55, 56] Its purpose is to accelerate healing-and-repair processes in the gastrointestinal tract. Used therapeutically, BPC 157 has been shown to promote the healing of the GI tract, as well as most other tissues, including muscles, ligaments, tendons, bone, organs such as the brain, spinal cord, and so forth. It has also been shown to promote wound healing and is being investigated as a therapy for various central nervous system disorders through its effect on the gut–brain axis. While all these applications will likely be beneficial in cats, the most promising immediate use would be for chronic gastrointestinal conditions, such as inflammatory bowel disease, as well as for the soreness, aches, and pains associated with injury and aging. BPC 157 can be administered orally for GI-related issues or as an injection for musculoskeletal or other concerns.

Thymosin Beta 4

Thymosin beta 4 is a peptide produced by all tissues and cells in the body. Similar to BPC 157, thymosin beta 4 has tissue-regeneration properties and has been shown to have regenerative effects in the heart, liver, and eye, and in wound healing. Because of its ability to mobilize stem cells in the body, it is also being evaluated as a primary therapy for longevity.[57, 58, 59, 60, 61]

There is a degree of controversy surrounding thymosin beta-4. It has been suggested that some cancer cells overexpress thymosin beta 4, raising concerns that administering it could promote cancer. The research evidence here is not strong, and there is also research to suggest the opposite, but nonetheless it is concerning for some people.[62, 63, 64] In response to these concerns, fragments of thymosin beta 4 can be used rather than the entire peptide. The full compound consists of 43 amino acids. It has been found that the fragment containing amino acids 1–4 is anti-inflammatory and the one containing 17–23 promotes tissue healing. There is no evidence to connect the fragments to cancer. Thymosin beta 4, or fragments thereof, is administered via injection, most commonly for immune system support, to decrease inflammation, and for tissue generation and the promotion of longevity.

CJC 1295 + Ipamorelin

The story of CJC 1295 and ipamorelin is really the story of growth hormone (GH). GH is produced in the pituitary gland at the base of the brain, and as the name would suggest, it plays a large role in growth and development.[65, 66, 67] It stimulates bone and muscle growth, regulating body fat levels, and even brain development and function. As our cats get older, levels of GH naturally decline. This is one of the major reasons why muscle mass decreases and body fat tends to increase with advancing age.

In the human longevity space, there are treatment protocols where people receive human growth hormone (HGH). There is, however, some concern that long-term use of HGH could lead to problems such as the onset of diabetes or cancer. Most longevity doctors prefer to encourage the body to produce its own GH through the use of peptides, rather than giving GH directly. CJC 1295 and ipamorelin are used, almost always in combination, to stimulate production of GH from the pituitary gland. Indications for use include building muscle, decreasing body fat, and facilitating healing of injuries, as well as increasing sleep quality and cognitive function. CJC 1295 and ipamorelin are administered via injection.

* * *

As you can see, there are quite a few regenerative treatments available for cats and even more in the "coming soon" category. These technological advances are going to have a large impact on the health and longevity of our current—and future—pets, and with more and more longevity-focused options becoming available, one of the facets of animal health that will turn out to be increasingly important will be our ability to monitor health in real time. This emerging technology will become indispensable to supporting animal health, and it is the topic of the upcoming chapter.

CHAPTER 8

TRACKING HEALTH

If you have read all the chapters to this point, you know more about longevity medicine than most veterinarians and physicians. This is cutting-edge information much of the medical community has yet to embrace. The final piece of the longevity puzzle is addressing the single greatest challenge of veterinary medicine and animal health in general: How do you know when your pet is sick?

In this chapter I'll alert you to some of the warning signs of a sick cat and teach you how to be more mindful of subtle changes. I'll also introduce some potential new technologies that could really help when it comes to early detection of health issues.

OUR LYING BEST FRIENDS

As nonverbal patients, animals can't tell us when something is wrong. But the challenge we face goes even deeper. Not only can they not communicate to us verbally when something is wrong, but they flat-out won't communicate this at all. Our cats are 100 percent honest with this one exception, and the reason is simple: an animal in the wild that looks sick or injured becomes a target for predators. Despite tens of thousands of years of domestication, our cats are still hardwired to make it look like everything is okay, even when it isn't.

The practical result of our cats lying to us about not feeling well is that by the time they look sick, they probably have been sick for a while. This leads to delays in seeking medical care and late-stage diagnoses. You don't need to have an advanced degree in medicine to understand that making a diagnosis when a disease is in an advanced stage leads to fewer treatment options and, sadly, poorer outcomes.

This inability to diagnose problems early has plagued cat owners and veterinarians since there have been cat owners and veterinarians. Chances are pretty good you have had a personal experience with a cat where a problem was diagnosed much later than you would have preferred. As a veterinarian, I deal with this every day. People frequently will say, "He was fine last week." The truth is, he wasn't, but he wanted you to think he was.

It would be easy to say the answer here is that as cat parents, we all need to be more observant. There is some truth to this statement, and certainly one of the key early indicators of a problem in a cat is a change in their routine. You see, cats like routine. They eat at the same time every day, they wake up and go to sleep with consistency, and their playtime is generally regular as well. When you see your cat changing their routine without an obvious reason, it is a signal for you to pay close attention. Changes might be subtle, such as eating slower or not wanting breakfast until a little later than normal. They may be drinking more water than usual or sleeping more or sleeping in different places than they typically do. Perhaps they aren't as interested in playtime. *Any change in their routine can be an early indicator of a medical problem.* When in doubt, contact your veterinarian. If your gut tells you there is something wrong, be persistent and get your cat seen and evaluated.

Being more attentive and recognizing subtle changes in behavior is an important step toward earlier diagnosis. That said, sometimes the changes may be too subtle to notice, they may occur when you are not in the house, or none may be present at all. We need to find a better, more reliable way to get clued into medical problems as early as possible. Finding the solution to the nonverbal, symptom-hiding cat is not simple, but it is attainable. In essence, we have to figure out how to "listen" in ways we never have before.

A NEW WAY TO LISTEN

You have undoubtedly heard of wearable devices for people, such as Fitbit, Apple Watch, WHOOP, or Oura Ring, among others. These devices monitor biometric parameters, such as heart rate, heart rhythm, and pulse oximetry. This data is then utilized to provide insight into the wearer's health. If you have a wearable device, you are seeing things like "sleep scores," "recovery scores," heart rate variability, calories burned, and a host of other metrics that the device uses to monitor your health and well-being. It will give you insight into how effective your exercise is and even how much you should exercise on a given day based on how well you slept the night before. Having this window into how your body is working is pretty cool.

Allow me to recount a quick personal story: I have a wearable that I enjoy using for all of the above reasons. A while back, I woke up one morning and received an alert from the device's app on my phone that I had never seen before: my respiration rate overnight was higher than my average, and this is frequently a sign of a person getting sick. I felt fine that morning, but the next day I was COVID-positive.

So, my wearable effectively knew I had COVID the day before I began to feel sick. In other words, it didn't need anything from me in order to detect a problem. Consider this technology from an animal-health perspective. Let's say a cat owner receives a message on their phone saying that their cat's average heart rate and respiration rate have increased by 10 percent over the past day or two, and their activity level is down a little. Now, a 10 percent change in respiration is too subtle for even the most diligent cat owner to recognize, but these changes are almost certainly a sign of a problem. It could be the cat is in pain or has heart disease or any number of other things, and determining the specifics is where your veterinarian comes in. Being alerted to minute changes like these could avert a scenario where days, weeks, or even months later, there is a "hair on fire" trip to the emergency room that may not have a good ending. Being able to intervene before issues escalate is the key to more successful treatment outcomes.

Here is another real-world story: A while ago I received a text from a friend with a video clip of his cat. He said she was not acting right and wanted to know what I thought. I looked at the video, and she was clearly in respiratory distress. Given that my friend and his cat are in Southern California and I am up in NorCal, it wasn't anything I could personally attend to. I directed him to take his cat to the emergency clinic immediately, where she was diagnosed with congestive heart failure. Thankfully, she was treated and survived, but things could have easily gone the other way. If my friend had been alerted when his cat's respiration rate first began to elevate, his cat could have been diagnosed and treated before things became life-threatening.

ADVANTAGES OF BIOMETRIC MONITORING

In the near future, biometric monitoring in the form of wearables for cats on a collar or harness will become standard of care for people who want to be proactive with their cats' health. Coupled with the wearable, imagine an app that can tell you if your cat is getting the optimal amount of exercise, give you guidance on how much food they should be eating based on their health and activity level, and provide advice on medical concerns. Plus, all of this data would be sent to your veterinarian as well so they have the same window into your cat that you do. The entire point of this book is for you to learn how to intervene early when it comes to your cat's life span and health span. Wearables like these will, for the first time, put us in the driver's seat and allow us to get ahead of health problems before they become symptomatic.

By now, you are starting to see the diagnostic value in a device that can provide you with information about subtle changes in your cat's vital signs, and the applications don't stop there. The same device will be incredibly useful in monitoring treatment. Imagine your cat has arthritis and your veterinarian is providing treatment. If your cat's wearable shows their heart rate and respiration rate are down and activity level is up, that is a pretty good indication treatment is working. Conversely, if no changes are seen, then you know you have to try something else. A wearable could be used in exactly the same way to monitor efficacy of all the longevity-focused interventions we have discussed thus far.

Biometric wearables will actually become more effective the longer they are used, because the software and artificial intelligence (AI) will learn your cat's patterns and be even better able to predict problems with the slightest indication of change. This kind of data will, of course, be valuable for your individual cat, but it will also benefit the entire population of cats using wearables. The aggregate of tens or hundreds of thousands of cats providing input will help the AI learn more and faster, and eventually there will be known biometric patterns for specific diseases, breeds, ages, and so forth. The applications of this kind of data in both the patient-care and research arenas are staggering. Biometric wearable technology has the power to dramatically change animal health care, lower costs for pet owners, and promote longevity in our furry family members.

WHAT'S COMING NEXT?

You may be aware of some wearables for dogs currently on the market such as Whistle and Fi, although there really isn't anything out there for cats. Most of these canine wearables don't, however, monitor actual vital signs, and the few that do have limitations that make them impractical for daily home use. A typical device only measures movement through the use of an accelerometer and a GPS tracker. This is helpful in knowing how active your pet has been, and it can even be used to alert you if your pet has been scratching a lot and potentially if they have a seizure. In other words, these devices will give you some insight into your pet's health, but without vital-signs data, there is only so much these products can tell you.

Things would be easy if we could just take the technology used for wearables for people and apply it to cats. I'm sure you have already deduced the problem here—fur. Wearables for people collect data by being in direct contact with the skin. This allows a variety of sensors to detect what is happening in the wearer's body. If you take your

Apple Watch and place it on the top of your head, it won't work, because it can't read through your hair (assuming, of course, that you have hair).

So the key to a world-changing wearable for cats begins with noncontact vital-sign sensing. There are some technologies out there that are approaching these capabilities, and it is only a matter of time before you can go online and purchase one. If we look even a little further down the road, the evolution beyond wearables will be implantable technology. I'm sure you are familiar with microchips for cats. These chips, about the size of a grain of rice, encode a unique ID number that can be used to reunite a lost pet with their owner. A veterinarian or animal-services department simply waves a scanner over the cat and it provides the number, which is stored in a national database. When the chips are implanted, the owner registers their information with the chip number, so when we call with a chip number, they can tell us how to contact the owner. Contrary to what a lot of people seem to think, microchips cannot be used to track your cat. They can only be "read" by a scanner that is inches away from the microchip. Big Brother is definitely not watching you or your cat via their chip.

One interesting upgrade to microchips recently is that they can also tell your cat's body temperature. Pretty cool, right? As technology advances, it is likely these chips will have onboard sensors that can detect a range of biometric parameters, from heart rate to blood parameters like oxygenation and blood sugar, kidney function, and so forth. When this happens, it will be a sea change for the world of health care for both humans and animals. Talk about early diagnosis!

Whether the monitor is wearable or implantable, the purpose of the sensor is really only to feed information to the artificial-intelligence systems that will perform the real magic. Artificial intelligence, machine learning, and neural nets are already changing the world, as computer systems are now able to "learn." Just like we humans learn through our experiences, computer systems learn through data input. The more data you feed them, the more they learn. In the case of wearables for cats, the more cats there are wearing devices and the longer they wear them, the speedier the learning and the better the predictive accuracy of the software. When we reach the point where hundreds of thousands of cats have wearables, the amount of data collected will be enormous, and subsequently the power of the predictive algorithms will be immense! Wearable biometric monitors are in the "coming soon" category, and implantables are "coming later," but definitely keep an eye out. It won't be too long before wearables for both humans and animals will become as ubiquitous as cell phones, and dedicated pet owners wouldn't dream of having a cat without one.

How Can I Track My Cat's Health Right Now?

Our tools for health tracking for kitties now rely on an observant owner and a veterinarian's ability to run diagnostic tests such as blood work, X-rays, and so on. Owners can also weigh their cat on a regular schedule at home. All of these are great options, but they don't hold a candle to real-time vital-sign and activity monitoring when it comes to promoting health and longevity.

* * *

Wearable health monitors for cats will be the next evolution of their health care. When we combine this with all the other facets of care we have discussed that promote longevity, you can begin to see how we are going to be able to make a huge impact on both quality and quantity of life. The only thing left for us to do now is to take all this information and turn it into something actionable for you, as a pet parent.

CHAPTER 9

OVERVIEW AND SUMMARY OF RECOMMENDATIONS

By now, you have a familiarity with the hallmarks of aging and how various interventions can impact them and, ultimately, prolong your cat's life span and health span. The key to successfully implementing a longevity plan for your furry family members is creating one that will be effective and sustainable *for you.* If the plan is too complicated or expensive to adhere to, chances are that you won't keep up with it in the long term, so keep this in mind as you decide how to proceed.

What follows is a brief review of information from the previous chapters, which will help lay the groundwork by suggesting what to prioritize and ways to implement a longevity strategy for your cat. The prerequisite to success at anything is building a strong foundation. Using the pyramid of longevity as a model, let's break down what actions are recommended at each level. The lower the level, the more important and impactful your actions will be with respect to promoting longevity for your cat.

Remember, none of this is written in stone; feel free to make adjustments according to what works best for you and your cat. The point here is to implement strategies that are sustainable with regard to your time and resources. Even if diet and lifestyle are as much as you can take on, optimizing those will have an enormous impact on your cat's life.

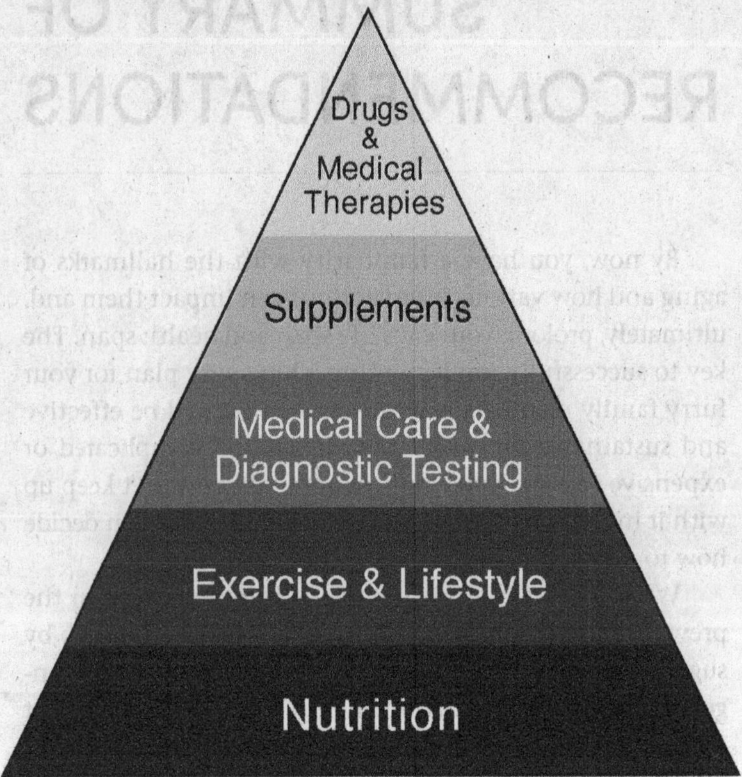

LEVEL 1: NUTRITION

It all starts here. Nutrition is the foundation of good health, full stop. Don't spend a minute or a dime on anything before you have optimized your cat's nutrition as much as you can. Think of nutrition and lifestyle as the tree upon which all the ornaments (diagnostics, supplements, drugs, and procedures) are hung. Strengthen the tree before you do anything else.

In principle, optimizing nutrition for your cat is easy. It is easier, in fact, than optimizing your own. You are in complete control of what your cat eats, and as such, you can make sure every bite of food they take is optimized. The goal is to get as close to a balanced, fresh, whole-food diet as possible.

Here is what you need to know:

- Foods can be commercially prepared in cooked, raw, or freeze-dried form, or they can be homemade from a balanced recipe.
- Balanced diets are important. At least 80 percent of your cat's food intake should be a balanced diet of nutritionally sound, healthy food that does not include treats.
- Rotate through different recipes over time to provide your cat with a spectrum of nutrients.
- Frequency of diet rotation depends on how easily your cat can adapt to the change. Once they are accustomed to a variety of foods, most don't require a transition from one to the next, but if your cat has a sensitive GI tract, consider doing a gradual transition from one recipe to another three to four times annually.

- Fresh-food diets are more expensive than kibble or canned. If you are unable to feed 100 percent balanced fresh foods, supplement fresh food on top of high-quality canned food or kibble.
- Do not overfeed—aim for a body condition score of 5 on a scale of 9 (see chart on page 74).
- If possible, feed once daily.

LEVEL 2: EXERCISE AND LIFESTYLE

Along with good nutrition, the benefits of exercise and lifestyle are intuitively obvious, although when it comes to cats, you do need to determine what is best for each as an individual based on their breed, temperament, and other factors. Keep in mind, exercise is about both physical and mental health. High-energy cats in particular need to work off some energy so they can be calm and relaxed. In addition, the *type* of exercise your cat gets is as important as the time spent exercising. Keep things interesting for your cat by initiating a variety of games and engaging them in lots of playtime like chasing a toy and hunting for treats. If you have more than one cat, chances are they are keeping themselves busy chasing each other around the house as well.

The other side of the coin here is lifestyle. Stress and anxiety of any kind are detrimental to good health. Clearly, life has its stressful moments for both cats and humans. This is more about your cat's day-to-day life, which should focus on them feeling safe and secure. A cat also feeds off their owner's emotional state. If you are a high-stress individual or live in a high-stress environment, both your cat's health and your own are likely being impacted. For both of your sakes, consider what it will take to turn down the heat and find ways for each of you to decompress. The foundation of a good lifestyle for cats is one that's compatible with yours.

Here are your guidelines:

- Regular, daily exercise is important for both you and your cat.
- The amount and type of exercise that is best varies based on age, breed, physical conditioning, and so forth.
- Understanding your cat's natural energy levels and personality will improve both their quality of life and yours.
- Having a stable home where your cat feels safe and secure promotes happiness and longevity. Cats enjoy consistency and routine.
- Cats have differing levels of sociability. Provide them with the level of social interaction that seems to work best for them and allow them some quiet downtime when they want it.

LEVEL 3: MEDICAL CARE AND DIAGNOSTIC TESTING

With regard to specific medical care, the biggest take-home here is that your job is to be an advocate for your cat, especially if you don't have access to a holistic or integrative veterinarian. This means asking questions (respectfully) when your veterinarian makes recommendations for vaccines, medications, surgeries, and so forth. For example, just because your cat is "due" for something doesn't necessarily mean it has to, or even should, happen, and not every infection requires oral antibiotics. Remember, ideal medical care is personalized to the individual animal, and no one protocol is appropriate for all cats. This is true for all facets of veterinary care.

As your cat's advocate, be on the lookout for changes in behavior. If your cat breaks their daily routine and there isn't a clear explanation why, you need to pay close attention. This is frequently the first sign of medical problems. The key to success with veterinary care is to be proactive. Don't wait until your cat is sick to get them looked at. An ounce of prevention really is worth a pound of cure.

For even greater insight into how your cat is doing, biometric wearables are the next big thing. Many of the current products can provide you with some data regarding your cat's activity level, but the next-generation devices on the horizon will monitor vital signs and utilize artificial intelligence to predict illness at its earliest stages. These wearables will revolutionize animal health and veterinary medicine in profound ways.

Dental care is critically important to health and longevity, and this is something that really is on you as your cat's caretaker. Yes, your veterinarian can clean your cat's teeth, but that usually necessitates general anesthesia, which is always a risk. Additionally, imagine if you had your teeth cleaned by your dentist and then you didn't brush them until your appointment the following year. That is what happens all the time with cats, and it leads to problems for middle-aged and older cats. You want to have a routine at home that includes brushing and all-natural dental chews.

The big advantage of diagnostic testing is that it allows us to be more objective about our longevity plan for our cats. There certainly are facets of our strategy that can, and should, be implemented regardless of test results. There are other facets that we do not yet have the ability to test for. That said, measuring specific parameters that affect aging allows us to implement therapies and subsequently observe their effects. Few things in health care are one-size-fits-all, and an intervention that works for one cat may not work for another. By utilizing diagnostic testing, we can determine how well our treatments are working and, most important, when they are *not* working, so we can try more or different therapeutics.

Some tests—complete blood count and blood chemistries—can easily be run by your veterinarian. Some tests—profiling genetic predispositions for disease (Basepaws) and food sensitivity (NutriScan)—can be done at home if your veterinarian doesn't offer them. Other diagnostics—vitamin and mineral levels, omega fatty acid levels, cancer screening, and age profiles such as DNA methylation and telomere testing—require blood samples, yet are frequently not offered by most veterinarians. But with the information provided in Chapter 2, you may be able to convince your veterinarian to help you submit these to the appropriate labs.

One other note about diagnostic testing: There is definitely value in monitoring parameters of health and longevity that we have some control over and can take action on if the testing indicates it is necessary. That said, testing costs money, and for the most part, so do longevity-based treatments. The one thing we can say for sure is that money spent on testing will not directly help our cats live better or longer. If there is a question of where to allocate finances, always prioritize treatment over diagnostics whenever possible.

Here are some guidelines to follow:

- Vaccines are necessary and beneficial, but overvaccination is dangerous. It is important to understand the risk-benefit analysis for all vaccines and medications. Strictly indoor cats frequently do not require boosters after their kitten vaccines.
- Ideally, spay or neuter cats around six months of age, although many kittens from shelters will be spayed or neutered earlier.
- If your cat is indoors, flea-and-tick control is likely not necessary. If it becomes necessary, use an intervention until the problem is resolved and then discontinue.
- Pharmaceuticals such as antibiotics and anti-inflammatories are sometimes necessary, but they are overprescribed. Explore other options whenever possible.
- Regular examinations by your veterinarian can help detect medical problems early. Younger cats should be seen at least once per year, while middle-aged or older cats may benefit from two or three visits annually.
- Practice good oral health through regular dental care at home and, when necessary, with your veterinarian.
- Regular diagnostic testing in the form of blood, urine, and stool analysis is a valuable screening tool.

- Longevity-focused testing such as genetic screening, vitamin levels, inflammatory markers, and so forth provides great insight into how to best implement longevity therapies in levels 4 and 5.
- Get pet insurance early so you never have to make major medical decisions based on cost.

LEVEL 4: SUPPLEMENTS

Diet, lifestyle, exercise, and thoughtful medical care are all critical components of your cat's longevity. As we move into supplements, we are entering a different realm of longevity science. We are leveraging our knowledge of the hallmarks of aging and strategically incorporating supplements to hack into our cats' biology and allow their bodies to function better and longer. This is where things get really interesting . . .

Supplements for longevity are easily accessible and are generally very safe. Do your best to create a protocol that is both effective and sustainable on your end. Don't try to give your cat everything at once! There are combination supplements on the market that will allow you to check off multiple compounds on the list by giving a single product. This can make life a bit easier. Certain supplements, like omega fatty acids, are beneficial to give over the long term. Most others are better given for a period of time and then rotated out in exchange for different ones. This allows the body to benefit from accessing different pathways and mechanisms to positively affect the hallmarks of aging over time.

Here are some suggested guidelines for longevity supplementation:

Supplements you can give every day for the long term:

- Probiotics
  - These may include pre- and/or postbiotics.
  - Rotate through different products at least a few times annually.
- Omega fatty acids
  - Focus particularly on EPA and DHA found in marine oils.
  - If possible, check omega fatty acid levels through a blood test to ensure ideal levels of supplementation.
- Vitamins and minerals
  - Use formulas made for cats, when available.
  - It's okay to rotate through different products over time to provide a spectrum of nutrients and sources of ingredients.
  - If your pet is eating a balanced, fresh-food diet, a multivitamin may not be necessary.

Rotation strategy for other supplements:

- The goal is to cover multiple hallmarks of aging with only a few supplements. The table on page 144 identifies which hallmarks each supplement addresses.
- Rotate supplements every one to two months.

- It is not necessary to use everything on the list.
- Keep it simple: supplementing more than two or three things at any one time may become difficult to sustain, and/or your cat may not like it.

LEVEL 5: LONGEVITY-FOCUSED DRUGS AND MEDICAL THERAPIES

Accessibility and financial concerns are paramount when you consider longevity interventions at this level. When it comes to these kinds of treatments, always consult with a veterinarian before starting anything.

These therapies are changing the environment within your cat's body in ways that would otherwise be impossible. Having said that, these actions at the top of the pyramid require more of a financial commitment. While pet insurance generally will pay for treating a specific medical condition, they probably are not going to cover therapies being used to support longevity.

In addition to the cost considerations, many of the therapies and interventions described in Chapter 7 may not be readily available in your area. These are specialized therapies that, honestly, you would probably have a hard time finding if you needed to get *yourself* treated. If one or more of the treatments described are available for your cat, speak with the veterinarian providing the service about how your cat could best benefit.

To be clear, you can make an enormous impact on your cat's longevity without ever utilizing even one of these therapies, but I wanted to shine the light on every option that is currently available or forthcoming. As with everything else, whatever you do, it has to be sustainable for both you and your cat. I would much rather see people focus their efforts and resources toward feeding an optimal diet and creating an ideal lifestyle for their cat than spend all their money on high-tech interventions. You must establish the foundation for optimal health before you do anything else.

Here are some suggestions on how best to utilize these therapies if they are available to you:

- *Hyperbaric oxygen therapy:* While a study evaluating HBOT and telomere length in humans showed positive results, it required daily treatments for 60 days, and there has yet to be a veterinary-equivalent study. There is every reason to believe that HBOT benefits cats the same way it does humans, and there are no drawbacks besides the potential cost. It may be possible for you to have your cat treated weekly or monthly for the long term, which might be helpful with supporting tissue repair and good health. Home-use hyperbaric chambers are available for purchase, but these are impractical because they pressurize with room air and require the user to wear an oxygen mask while in the chamber. In my experience, this is not something a cat will tolerate, so a chamber that pressurizes with oxygen, such as one found in a medical facility, will be necessary. Consult with a veterinarian familiar with HBOT to discuss the specific protocol.
- *Ozone therapy:* Ozone therapy at regular intervals is likely to provide health benefits for cats. Ozone can be administered in a variety

of ways, including via injection, through ozonated water, and even rectally. If your veterinarian offers ozone, consider having your cat treated every four to eight weeks. Like HBOT, there are home units available for purchase that give ozone gas rectally. Some people do this for their own longevity, and you can provide it for your cat as well. Consult with a veterinarian familiar with ozone to discuss the specifics of how to do this safely for your cat.

- *Platelet-rich plasma:* PRP definitively requires a veterinarian, and generally I would only suggest it for the treatment of an injury, such as damage to a ligament, tendon, muscle, or joint.
- *Mesenchymal stem cell therapy:* Conventional stem cell therapy has applications in treating the same spectrum of injuries as PRP. As discussed in Chapter 7, the size of mesenchymal stem cells makes them impractical for IV administration, and thus they are not the best choice as an overall longevity therapy.
- *Very small embryonic-like stem cells:* VSELs are new to veterinary medicine and aren't even widely known in human medicine. The preliminary evidence we have so far indicates they can be used in the treatment of injuries like those mentioned above, as well as certain types of organ dysfunction like heart disease, brain and spinal cord conditions, and so forth. In addition, VSELs appear to be applicable as

an overall longevity therapy, and anecdotally, human patients who have been treated with VSELs have decreased their epigenetic ages as measured through DNA methylation. The originator of therapeutic VSELs, Dr. Todd Ovokaitys, treats his human patients quarterly to promote longevity. As of now, there are only a handful of veterinarians who are able to offer VSEL therapy for their patients. If you and your cat are in the San Francisco Bay Area, give me a call.

- *Microbiome restorative therapy:* MBRT, more commonly known as fecal transplantation, is typically used for patients with chronic GI issues, such as inflammatory bowel disease, colitis, dysbiosis, and so on. From a longevity perspective, there may be benefits to transplanting stool from a younger animal into an older one. This is the kind of thing that could be done once or twice annually. I probably don't have to say this, *but don't try this at home.* Donor animals should be carefully selected based on lifestyle, medication history, and diet, and their stool must be screened to ensure it is free of pathogens. Do this only through your veterinarian.
- *Rapamycin:* As pharmaceuticals go, rapamycin appears to have the greatest potential as a longevity drug, and while there is ongoing research into its effects on dogs, we don't know too much regarding cats just yet. Rapamycin should only be used intermittently,

as long-term inhibition of the mTOR pathway is potentially harmful. Administer this only under direct veterinary supervision.

- *Dasatinib:* Dasatinib is a potent senolytic and thus probably could be useful in an overall longevity plan for cats. While it has been studied for cats with cancer, there are no published longevity-specific feline studies. Recall that dasatinib is also a chemotherapy drug, so don't take its use lightly. Like rapamycin, it should be used intermittently and only under direct veterinary supervision.
- *Peptides:* Peptides are exciting because they are a broad class of compounds that show a lot of potential to promote healing and longevity. In addition, they can be administered at home by pet owners. Depending on the peptide, they may be oral or injectable. As a rule, peptides are given in cycles and are frequently stacked, meaning that more than one peptide is given per cycle. Cycles generally last from one to three months. Even though this is something you can do at home, definitely consult with a veterinarian prior to implementing peptide therapy.

CONCLUSIONS . . . BUT NOT THE END

Before you started reading this book, you may have thought of aging as an unstoppable force. That would be understandable, since during the entire history of the world, that has been the case. With an understanding of the hallmarks of aging, however, we have shone a light onto mechanisms that can be used to stop the unstoppable. Consider this: A little over 100 years ago, the concept of riding in a machine that can fly would have been considered ludicrous. Now millions of people fly every day. A little over 50 years ago, the idea of space travel was the stuff of H. G. Wells and other science-fiction writers. Now we have space tourism and asteroid mining. Things that once seemed impossible have a way of not only becoming possible but also unremarkable. Yesterday's miracles are today's mundane occurrences. Extending life span is just one more of these things.

The information provided in these chapters represents most of what current longevity science has to say and offer to people in search of longer and better lives for themselves and their cats. As much information as was presented here, the field of longevity science is in its earliest stages. Renowned futurist Ray Kurzweil predicts human longevity will reach "escape velocity" by approximately 2030. This means we will be able to turn the clock back faster than we are chronologically aging. In other words, people—and presumably animals like cats—will no longer have to age and may even be able to do so in reverse and get younger!

The best course of action right now is to utilize the information in this book to keep your cat as healthy and happy as possible. Create the best life you can for the both of you, and you may find you are able to extend your cat's quality and quantity of life. Depending on how old your cat is now, the two of you may reach escape velocity together!

RESOURCES

Lifespan: Why We Age—and Why We Don't Have To, by David Sinclair

Super Human: The Bulletproof Plan to Age Backward and Maybe Even Live Forever, by Dave Asprey

The Energy Formula: Six Life Changing Ingredients to Unleash Your Limitless Potential, by Shawn Wells

Why You Are Still Sick: How Infections Can Break Your Immune System & How You Can Recover, by Gary Kaplan and Donna Beech

The Ultimate Pet Health Guide: Breakthrough Nutrition and Integrative Care for Dogs and Cats, by Gary Richter

* * *

Ultimate Pet Nutrition: www.ultimatepetnutrition.com

ENDNOTES

Chapter 1

1. "Oldest cat ever," *Guinness Book of World Records,* April 19, 2023, https://www.guinnessworldrecords.com/world-records/oldest-cat-ever.
2. M. Gannon, "China's first emperor ordered official search for immortality elixir," *Live Science,* December 27, 2017, https://www.livescience.com/61286-first-chinese-emperor-sought-immortality.html.
3. C. López-Otín et al., "The hallmarks of aging," *Cell* 153, no. 6 (June 6, 2013): 1194–1217, https://www.ncbi.nlm.nih.gov/pmc/articles/PMC3836174.
4. T. Schmauck-Medina et al., "New hallmarks of ageing: a 2022 Copenhagen ageing meeting summary," *Aging* (Albany, NY) 14, no. 16 (August 29, 2022): 6829–39, https://doi.org/10.18632/ aging.204248.
5. S. Horvath and K. Raj, "DNA methylation-based biomarkers and the epigenetic clock theory of ageing," *Nature Reviews Genetics* 19 (2018): 371–84, https://www.nature.com/articles/s41576-018-0004-3.
6. L. Fontana, L. Partridge, and V. D. Longo, "Extending healthy life span—from yeast to humans," *Science* 328 (2010): 321–26.
7. D. Papadopoli et al., "mTOR as a central regulator of lifespan and aging," *F1000Research* 8 (July 2, 2019): F1000 Faculty Rev-998, https://www.ncbi.nlm.nih.gov/pmc/articles/PMC6611156.
8. T. Wilmanski et al., "Gut microbiome pattern reflects healthy ageing and predicts survival in humans," *Nature Metabolism* 3, no. 2 (February 2021): 274–86, https://doi.org/10.1038/ s42255-021-00348-0.
9. *Merriam-Webster,* s.v. "disease (n.)," accessed 15 June 2022, https:// www.merriam-webster.com/dictionary/disease.

Chapter 2

1. "The Human Genome Project," About Genomics, National Human Genome Research Institute, updated September 2, 2022, https://www. genome.gov/human-genome-project.
2. M. J. Berridge, "Vitamin D deficiency accelerates ageing and age-related diseases: a novel hypothesis," *Journal of Physiology* 595, no. 22 (2017): 6825–36, https://doi.org/10.1113/JP274887.

3. Z. Zou et al., "Magnesium in aging and aging-related disease," *STEMedicine* 3, no. 2 (2022): e119, https://doi.org/10.37175/stemedicine.v3i2.119.

4. E. E. Bitter et al., "Thymidine kinase 1 through the ages: a comprehensive review," *Cell & Bioscience* 10, no. 138 (November 27, 2020), https://doi.org/10.1186/s13578-020-00493-1.

5. W. J. Dodds, "Diagnosis of feline food sensitivity and intolerance using saliva: 1000 cases," *Animals* (Basel) 9, no. 8 (August 6, 2019): 534, https://doi.org/10.3390/ani9080534.

6. S. P. Wiertsema et al., "The interplay between the gut microbiome and the immune system in the context of infectious diseases throughout life and the role of nutrition in optimizing treatment strategies," *Nutrients* 13, no. 3 (March 9, 2021): 886, https://doi .org/10.3390/nu13030886.

7. "Unique gut microbiome patterns linked to healthy aging, increased longevity," Research Highlights, National Institute on Aging, National Institutes of Health, Bethesda, MD, May 13, 2021, https://www.nia.nih.gov/news/unique-gut-microbiome-patterns-linked-healthy-aging-increased-longevity.

8. R. M. Buckley et al., "A new domestic cat genome assembly based on long sequence reads empowers feline genomic medicine and identifies a novel gene for dwarfism," *PLoS Genetics* 16, no. 10 (October 22, 2020): e1008926, https://doi.org/10.1371/journal .pgen.1008926.

9. M. I. McBurney et al., "Using an erythrocyte fatty acid fingerprint to predict risk of all-cause mortality: the Framingham Offspring Cohort," *American Journal of Clinical Nutrition* 114, no. 4 (2021): 1447–54, https://doi.org/10.1093/ajcn/nqab195.

10. A. D. Romano et al., "Oxidative stress and aging," *Journal of Nephrology* 23, suppl.15 (September–October 2010): S29–36.

11. W. J. Dodds, "Biomarkers of oxidative stress in dogs," *Medical Research Archives* 8, no. 5 (May 2020), https://esmed.org/MRA/mra/article/view/2112/193545570.

12. A. Vaiserman and D. Krasnienkov, "Telomere length as a marker of biological age: state-of-the-art, open issues, and future perspectives," *Frontiers in Genetics* 11 (January 21, 2021): 630186, https://doi .org/10.3389/fgene.2020.630186.

13. N. E. Braverman and A. B. Moser, "Functions of plasmalogen lipids in health and disease," *Biochimica et Biophysica Acta*1822, no. 9 (September 2012): 1442–52, https://doi.org/10.1016/j .bbadis.2012.05.008.

14. Z. A. Almsherqi, "Potential role of plasmalogens in the modulation of biomembrane morphology," *Frontiers in Cell and Developmental Biology* (July 21, 2021), https://www.frontiersin.org/articles/10.3389/fcell.2021.673917/full.

15. X. Q. Su, J. Wang, and A. J. Sinclair, "Plasmalogens and Alzheimer's disease: a review," *Lipids in Health and Disease* 18, no. 100 (2019), https://doi.org/10.1186/s12944-019-1044-1.

16. I. Pradas et al., "Exceptional human longevity is associated with a specific plasma phenotype of ether lipids," *Redox Biology* 21 (2019): 101127, https://doi.org/10.1016/j.redox.2019.101127.

17. T. Kimura et al., "Plasmalogen loss caused by remodeling deficiency in mitochondria," *Life Science Alliance* 2, no. 4 (August 21, 2019): e201900348, https://doi.org/10.26508/lsa.201900348.

18. M. Raffaele and M. Vinciguerra, "The costs and benefits of senotherapeutics for human health," *Lancet Healthy Longevity* 3 (2022): e67–e77, https://www.thelancet.com/pdfs/journals/lanhl/PIIS2666-7568(21)00300-7.pdf.

19. R. J. Pignolo et al., "Reducing senescent cell burden in aging and disease," *Trends in Molecular Medicine* 26, no. 7 (July 2020): 630–38, https://doi.org/10.1016/j.molmed.2020.03.005.

20. L. Mingus, "Common cancers in cats," Flint Animal Cancer Center, Colorado State University, November 20, 2019, https://www.csuanimalcancercenter.org/2019/11/20/common-cancers-in-cats/#:~:text=One%20in%20five%20cats%20will,lives%20after%20a%20cancer%20diagnosis.

21. A. Flory et al., "Clinical validation of a next-generation sequencing-based multi-cancer early detection 'liquid biopsy' blood test in over 1,000 dogs using an independent testing set: the CANcer Detection in Dogs (CANDiD) study," *PLoS One* 17, no. 4 (2022): e0266623, https://journals.plos.org/plosone/article?id=10.1371/journal .pone.0266623.

Chapter 3

1. C. A. Driscoll et al., "The Near Eastern origin of cat domestication," *Science* 317, no. 5837 (July 27, 2007): 519–23, https://doi.org/10.1126/science.1139518.

2. B. N. Ames, "Low micronutrient intake may accelerate the degenerative diseases of aging through allocation of scarce micronutrients by triage," *Proceedings of the National Academy of Sciences* 103, no. 47 (November 21, 2006): 17589–17594, https://www.pnas.org/doi/10.1073/pnas.0608757103.

3. C. Copat et al., "Heavy metals concentrations in fish and shellfish from eastern Mediterranean Sea: consumption advisories," *Food and Chemical Toxicology* 53 (March 2013): 33–37, https://doi.org/10.1016/j.fct.2012.11.038.

4. Z. Petrovic et al., "Meat production and consumption: environmental consequences," *Procedia Food Science* 5 (2015): 235–38, https://www.sciencedirect.com/science/article/pii/S2211601X15001315.

5. G. S. Okin, "Environmental impacts of food consumption by dogs and cats," *PLoS One* 12, no. 8 (2017): e0181301, https://journals .plos. org/plosone/article?id=10.1371/journal.pone.0181301.

6. T. Luntz, "U.S. drinking water widely contaminated," *Scientific American*, December 14, 2009, https://www.scientificamerican.com/ article/tap-drinking-water-contaminants-pollutants.

7. E. Bedford, "U.S. pet market sales by category 2018–2021," *Statista*, September 8, 2022, https://www.statista.com/statistics/253983/ pet-market-sales-in-the-us-by-category.

8. T. Wall, "Decade-long fresh, raw pet food sales growth trend," *PetFoodIndustry.com*, December 17, 2021, https://www .petfoodindustry.com/articles/10892-decade-long-fresh-raw-pet -food-sales-growth-trend?v=preview#:~:text=In%20Packaged%20Facts'%20 most%20recent,U.S.%20pet%20food%20retail%20sales.

9. N. Tamanna and N. Mahmood, "Food processing and Maillard reaction products: effect on human health and nutrition," *International Journal of Food Science* 3 (2015): 1–6, https://doi .org/10.1155/2015/526762.

10. D. Schroter and A. Hohn, "Role of advanced glycation end products in carcinogenesis and their therapeutic implications," *Current Pharmaceutical Design* 24, no. 44 (2018): 5245–51, https://doi.org/10.2 174/1381612825666190130145549.

11. G. Richter, *The Ultimate Pet Health Guide: Breakthrough Nutrition and Integrative Care for Dogs and Cats* (Carlsbad, CA: Hay House, 2017), 38.

12. R. Weindruch and R. S. Sohal, "Seminars in medicine of the Beth Israel Deaconess Medical Center. Caloric intake and aging," *New England Journal of Medicine* 337, no. 14 (1997): 986–94, https://doi .org/10.1056/NEJM199710023371407.

13. V. Adams et al., "Exceptional longevity and potential determinants of successful ageing in a cohort of 39 Labrador retrievers: results of a prospective longitudinal study," *Acta veterinaria Scandinavica* 58, no. 1 (May 11, 2016), https://doi.org/10.1186/s13028-016-0206-7.

14. A. K. Shetty et al., "Emerging anti-aging strategies—scientific basis and efficacy," *Aging and Disease* 9, no. 6 (December 4, 2018): 1165–84, https://www.ncbi.nlm.nih.gov/pmc/articles/PMC6284760.

15. E. E. Bray et al., "Once-daily feeding is associated with better health in companion dogs: results from the Dog Aging Project," *GeroScience* 44 (April 28, 2022): 1779–90, https://doi.org/10.1007/ s11357-022-00575-7.

16. A. Camara et al., "The daytime feeding frequency affects appetite-regulating hormones, amino acids, physical activity, and respiratory quotient, but not energy expenditure, in adult cats fed regimens for 21 days," *PLoS One* 15, no. 9 (September 18, 2020): e0238522, https:// doi.org/10.1371/journal.pone.0238522.

Chapter 4

1. C. Youngerman, "Cats: indoors or outdoors?," Health Topics, UC Davis Veterinary Medicine, April 8, 2019, https://healthtopics.vetmed.ucdavis.edu/health-topics/feline/cats-indoors-or-outdoors#:~:text=Indoor%20cats%20live%20on%20average,and%20protection%20from%20environmental%20hazards.
2. S. M. L. Tan, A. C. Stellato, and L. Niel, "Uncontrolled outdoor access for cats: an assessment of risks and benefits," *Animals* (Basel) 10, no. 2 (February 6, 2020): 258, https://doi.org/10.3390/ani10020258.
3. K. T. Teng et al., "Strong associations of nine-point body condition scoring with survival and lifespan in cats," *Journal of Feline Medicine and Surgery* 20, no. 12 (December 2018): 1110–18, https://doi.org/10.1177/1098612X17752198.
4. M. Venturelli, F. Schena, and R. S. Richardson, "The role of exercise capacity in the health and longevity of centenarians," *Maturitas* 73, no. 2 (October 2012): 115–20, https://doi.org/10.1016/j.maturitas.2012.07.009.
5. L. Mandolesi et al., "Effects of physical exercise on cognitive functioning and wellbeing: biological and psychological benefits," *Frontiers in Psychology* 9 (April 27, 2018): 509, https://doi.org/10.3389/fpsyg.2018.00509.
6. A. Rebelo-Marques et al., "Aging hallmarks: the benefits of physical exercise," *Frontiers in Endocrinology* (Lausanne) 9 (May 25, 2018): 258, https://doi.org/10.3389/fendo.2018.00258.
7. A. I. Qureshi et al., "Cat ownership and the risk of fatal cardiovascular diseases. Results from the second National Health and Nutrition Examination Study Mortality Follow-up Study," *Journal of Vascular Interventional Neurology* 2, no. 1 (January 2009): 132–35, https://www.ncbi.nlm.nih.gov/pmc/articles/PMC3317329.
8. N. J. Needell and N. Mehta-Naik, "Is pet ownership helpful in reducing the risk and severity of geriatric depression?," *Geriatrics* (Basel) 1, no. 4 (October 4, 2016): 24, https://doi.org/geriatrics1040024.
9. "The happiness of pet owners: new study reveals the happiest pet owners," How To Be Happy, Case Studies & Surveys, Tracking Happiness, updated April 18, 2022, https://www.trackinghappiness.com/happiness-of-pet-owners-study.
10. L. O. Lee et al., "Optimism is associated with exceptional longevity in 2 epidemiologic cohorts of men and women," *Proceedings of the National Academy of Sciences* 116, no 37 (September 10, 2019): 18357–62, https://doi.org/10.1073/pnas.1900712116.

Chapter 5

1. "Vaccines and sarcomas: a concern for cat owners," American Veterinary Medical Association, accessed 15 June 2022, https://www.avma.org/resources-tools/pet-owners/petcare/vaccines-and-sarcomas-concern-cat-owners#:~:text=Injection%2Dsite%20sarcomas%20are%20considered,per%2010%2C000%20to%2030%2C000%20vaccinations.
2. L. M. T. Dicks, S. M. Deane, and M. J. Grobbelaar, "Could the COVID-19-driven increased use of ivermectin lead to incidents of imbalanced gut microbiota and dysbiosis?," *Probiotics and Antimicrobial Proteins* 14, no. 2 (April 2022): 217–23, https://doi .org/10.1007/s12602-022-09925-5.
3. M. Levy et al., "Dysbiosis and the immune system," *Nature Reviews Immunology* 17, no. 4 (April 2017): 219–32, https://doi.org/10.1038/nri.2017.7.
4. G. A. Weiss and T. Hennet, "Mechanisms and consequences of intestinal dysbiosis," *Cellular and Molecular Life Sciences* 74, no. 16 (August 2017): 2959–77, https://doi.org/10.1007/s00018-017-2509-x.
5. S. R. Urfer et al., "Risk factors associated with lifespan in pet dogs evaluated in primary care veterinary hospitals," *Journal of the American Animal Hospital Association* 55, no. 3 (May/June 2019): 130–37, https://doi.org/10.5326/JAAHA-MS-6763.
6. Y. Watanabe et al., "Oral health for achieving longevity," *Geriatrics & Gerontology International* 20, no. 6 (June 2020): 526–38, https://doi.org/10.1111/ggi.13921.
7. Y. Heianza et al., "Duration and life-stage of antibiotic use and risks of all-cause and cause-specific mortality: prospective cohort study," *Circulation Research* 126, no. 3 (January 31, 2020): 364–73, https://doi.org/10.1161/CIRCRESAHA.119.315279.

Chapter 6

1. V. Raguraman and J. Subramaniam, "*Withania somnifera* root extract enhances telomerase activity in the human HeLa cell line," *Advances in Bioscience and Biotechnology* 7, no. 4 (April 2016), https://www.researchgate.net/publication/301295944_Withania_somnifera_Root_Extract_Enhances_Telomerase_Activity_in_the_Human_HeLa_Cell_Line.
2. R. Guo et al., "Withaferin A prevents myocardial ischemia/reperfusion injury by upregulating AMP-activated protein kinase-dependent B-cell lymphoma2 signaling," *Circulation Journal* 83, no. 8 (July 25, 2019): 1726–36, https://doi.org/10.1253/circj.CJ-18-1391.
3. S. Koduru et al., "Notch-1 inhibition by Withaferin-A: a therapeutic target against colon carcinogenesis," *Molecular Cancer Therapeutics* 9, no. 1 (2010): 202–10, https://doi.org/10.1158/1535-7163 .MCT-09-0771.

4. M. F. McCarty, "AMPK activation—protean potential for boosting healthspan," *AGE* 36, no. 2 (April 2014): 641–63, https://doi .org/10.1007/s11357-013-9595-y.

5. Y. Dang et al., "Berberine ameliorates cellular senescence and extends the lifespan of mice via regulating p16 and cyclin protein expression," *Aging Cell* 19, no. 1 (2020): e13060, https://doi .org/10.1111/acel.13060.

6. T. Nordström et al., "Associations between circulating carotenoids, genomic instability and the risk of high-grade prostate cancer," *The Prostate* 76, no. 4 (2016): 339–48, https://doi.org/10.1002/pros.23125.

7. D. Mantle and I. Hargreaves, "Coenzyme Q10 and degenerative disorders affecting longevity: an overview," *Antioxidants* (Basel) 8, no. 2 (February 16, 2019): 44, https://doi.org/10.3390/antiox8020044.

8. J. D. Hernández-Camacho et al., "Coenzyme Q_{10} supplementation in aging and disease," *Frontiers in Physiology* 4, no. 44 (February 5, 2018), https://www.frontiersin.org/articles/10.3389/fphys.2018.00044/full.

9. P. Shinde et al., "Curcumin restores the engraftment capacity of aged hematopoietic stem cells and also reduces PD-1 expression on cytotoxic T cells," *Journal of Tissue Engineering and Regenerative Medicine* 15, no. 4 (April 2021): 388–400, https://doi.org/10.1002/term.3180.

10. Z. Yang et al., "Curcumin-mediated bone marrow mesenchymal stem cell sheets create a favorable immune microenvironment for adult full-thickness cutaneous wound healing," *Stem Cell Research & Therapy* 9, no. 1 (January 31, 2018): 21, https://doi.org/10.1186/s13287-018-0768-6.

11. F. Mottola et al., "DNA damage in human amniotic cells: antigenotoxic potential of curcumin and α-lipoic acid," *Antioxidants* (Basel) 10, no. 7 (July 7, 2021): 1137, https://doi .org/10.3390/antiox10071137.

12. R. Sharma et al., "Long-term consumption of green tea EGCG enhances murine healthspan by mitigating multiple aspects of cellular senescence in mitotic and post-mitotic tissues, gut dysbiosis, and immunosenescence," *The Journal of Nutritional Biochemistry* 107 (May 23, 2022): 109068, https://doi.org/10.1016/j .jnutbio.2022.109068.

13. L. G. Xiong et al., "Epigallocatechin-3-gallate promotes healthy lifespan through mitohormesis during early-to-mid adulthood in Caenorhabditis elegans," *Redox Biology* 14 (2018): 305–15, https://doi. org/10.1016/j.redox.2017.09.019.

14. L. Yang et al., "The epigenetic modification of epigallocatechin gallate (EGCG) on cancer," *Current Drug Targets* 21, no. 11 (2020): 1099–1104, https://doi.org/10.2174/1389450121666200504080112.

15. H. Ding et al., "Epigallocatechin-3-gallate activates the AMP-activated protein kinase signaling pathway to reduce lipid accumulation in canine hepatocytes," *Journal of Cellular Physiology* 236, no. 1 (January 2021): 405–16, https://doi.org/10.1002/jcp.29869.

16. M. I. McBurney et al., "Using an erythrocyte fatty acid fingerprint to predict risk of all-cause mortality: the Framingham Offspring Cohort," *The American Journal of Clinical Nutrition* (October 2021): 1447–54, https://doi.org/10.1093/ajcn/nqab195.

17. R. Farzaneh-Far et al., "Association of marine omega-3 fatty acid levels with telomeric aging in patients with coronary heart disease," *JAMA* 303, no. 3 (2010): 250–57, https://doi.org/10.1001/jama.2009.2008.

18. C. M. Champigny et al., "Omega-3 monoacylglyceride effects on longevity, mitochondrial metabolism and oxidative stress: insights from Drosophila melanogaster," *Marine Drugs* 16, no. 11 (November 16, 2018): 453, https://doi.org/10.3390/md16110453.

19. U. N. Das, "'Cell membrane theory of senescence' and the role of bioactive lipids in aging, and aging associated diseases and their therapeutic implications," *Biomolecules* 11, no. 2 (February 8, 2021): 241, https://doi.org/10.3390/biom11020241.

20. F. Ponte et al., "Improvement of genetic stability in lymphocytes from Fanconi anemia patients through the combined effect of α-lipoic acid and N-acetylcysteine," *Orphanet Journal of Rare Diseases* 7 (May 16, 2012): 28, https://doi.org/10.1186/1750-1172-7-28.

21. Mottola et al., "DNA damage in human amniotic cells."

22. S. M. Dos Santos et al., "Mitochondrial dysfunction and alphalipoic acid: beneficial or harmful in Alzheimer's disease?," *Oxidative Medicine and Cellular Longevity* 2019 (November 30, 2019): 8409329, https://doi.org/10.1155/2019/8409329.

23. M. J. Yousefzadeh et al., "Fisetin is a senotherapeutic that extends health and lifespan," *eBioMedicine* 36 (October 2018): 18–28, https://doi.org/10.1016/j.ebiom.2018.09.015.

24. Z. Zou et al., "Magnesium in aging and aging-related disease," *STEMedicine* 3, no. 2 (2022): e119, https://doi.org/10.37175/stemedicine.v3i2.119.

25. G. A. Bubenik and S. J. Konturek, "Melatonin and aging: prospects for human treatment," *Journal of Physiology and Pharmacology* 62, no. 1 (February 2011): 13–19, https://pubmed.ncbi.nlm.nih .gov/21451205.

26. J. Fang et al., "Melatonin prevents senescence of canine adipose-derived mesenchymal stem cells through activating NRF2 and inhibiting ER stress," *Aging* 10, no. 10 (2018): 2954–72, https://doi .org/10.18632/aging.101602.

27. H. H. Peng et al., "*Ganoderma lucidum* stimulates autophagy-dependent longevity pathways in *Caenorhabditis elegans* and human cells," *Aging* 13, no. 10 (2021): 13474–95, https://doi.org/10.18632/aging.203068.

28. D. M. Ba et al., "Association of mushroom consumption with all-cause and cause-specific mortality among American adults: prospective cohort study findings from NHANES III," *Nutrition Journal* 20, no. 1 (April 22, 2021): 38, https://doi.org/10.1186/s12937-021-00691-8.

29. Z. A. Hamid et al., "The role of N-acetylcysteine supplementation on the oxidative stress levels, genotoxicity and lineage commitment potential of ex vivo murine haematopoietic stem/progenitor cells," *Sultan Qaboos University Medical Journal* 18, no. 2 (May 2018): e130–e136, https://doi.org/10.18295/squmj.2018.18.02.002.

30. D. J. Wright et al., "N-Acetylcysteine improves mitochondrial function and ameliorates behavioral deficits in the R6/1 mouse model of Huntington's disease," *Translational Psychiatry* 5, no. 1 (January 6, 2015): e492, https://doi.org/10.1038/tp.2014.131.

31. C. Shade, "The science behind NMN-A stable, reliable NAD+activator and anti-aging molecule," *Integrative Medicine* (Encinitas, CA) 19, no. 1 (February 2020): 12–14.

32. Tokushima University and Nature Research Custom Media, "Recent research into nicotinamide mononucleotide and ageing," Sponsor Feature, *Nature Portfolio*, https://www.nature.com/articles/d42473-022-00002-7.

33. S. Rigacci et al., "Oleuropein aglycone induces autophagy via the AMPK/mTOR signalling pathway: a mechanistic insight," *Oncotarget* 6, no. 34 (November 3, 2015): 35344–57, https://doi.org/10.18632/oncotarget.6119.

34. K. Cuanalo-Contreras and I. Moreno-Gonzalez, "Natural products as modulators of the proteostasis machinery: implications in neurodegenerative diseases," *International Journal of Molecular Sciences* 20, no. 19 (September 20, 2019): 4666, https://doi .org/10.3390/ijms20194666.

35. X. Q. Su, J. Wang, and A. J. Sinclair, "Plasmalogens and Alzheimer's disease: a review," *Lipids in Health and Disease* 18, no. 1 (April 16, 2019): 100, https://doi.org/10.1186/s12944-019-1044-1.

36. M. S. Hossain, S. Mawatari, and T. Fujino, "Biological functions of plasmalogens," *Advances in Experimental Medicine and Biology* 1299 (2020): 171–93, https://doi.org/10.1007/978-3-030-60204-8_13.

37. Z. A. Almsherqi, "Potential role of plasmalogens in the modulation of biomembrane morphology," *Frontiers in Cell and Developmental Biology* 9 (July 21, 2021): 673917, https://doi.org/10.3389/fcell.2021.673917.

38. X. Fang et al., "Evaluation of the anti-aging effects of a probiotic combination isolated from centenarians in a SAMP8 mouse model," *Frontiers in Immunology* 12 (December 2, 2021): 792746, https://doi .org/10.3389/fimmu.2021.792746.

39. W. L. Teng et al., "Pterostilbene attenuates particulate matter-induced oxidative stress, inflammation and aging in keratinocytes," *Antioxidants* (Basel) 10, no. 10 (September 29, 2021): 1552, https://doi.org/10.3390/antiox10101552.

40. K. W. Lange and S. Li, "Resveratrol, pterostilbene, and dementia," *BioFactors* 44, no. 1 (January 2018): 83–90, https://doi.org/10.1002/biof.1396.

41. J. M. Suárez-Rivero et al., "Pterostilbene in combination with mitochondrial cofactors improve mitochondrial function in cellular models of mitochondrial diseases," *Frontiers in Pharmacology* 13 (March 18, 2022): 862085, https://doi.org/10.3389/fphar.2022.862085.

42. T. Simpson, C. Kure, and C. Stough, "Assessing the efficacy and mechanisms of Pycnogenol® on cognitive aging from *in vitro* animal and human studies," *Frontiers in Pharmacology* 10 (July 3, 2019): 694, https://doi.org/10.3389/fphar.2019.00694.

43. P. Rohdewald, "Pleiotropic effects of French maritime pine bark extract to promote healthy aging," *Rejuvenation Research* 22, no. 3 (June 2019): 210–17, https://doi.org/10.1089/rej.2018.2095.

44. Z. H. Wei, Q. L. Peng, and B. H. Lau, "Pycnogenol enhances endothelial cell antioxidant defenses," *Redox Report* 3, no. 4 (August 1997): 219–24, https://doi.org/10.1080/13510002.1997.11747113.

45. M. Hosoi et al., "Pycnogenol® supplementation in minimal cognitive dysfunction," *Journal of Neurosurgical Sciences* 62, no. 3 (June 2018): 279–84, https://doi.org/10.23736/S0390-5616.18.04382-5.

46. E. J. Sohn et al., "Restoring effects of natural anti-oxidant quercetin on cellular senescent human dermal fibroblasts," *The American Journal of Chinese Medicine* 46, no. 4 (2018): 853–73, https://doi .org/10.1142/S0192415X18500453.

47. E. J. Novais et al., "Long-term treatment with senolytic drugs Dasatinib and Quercetin ameliorates age-dependent intervertebral disc degeneration in mice," *Nature Communications* 12, no. 1 (September 3, 2021): 5213, https://doi.org/10.1038/s41467-021-25453-2.

48. L. J. Hickson et al., "Senolytics decrease senescent cells in humans: preliminary report from a clinical trial of Dasatinib plus Quercetin in individuals with diabetic kidney disease," *eBioMedicine* 47 (September 2019): 446–56, https://doi.org/10.1016/j .ebiom.2019.08.069.

49. K. Cuanalo-Contreras and I. Moreno-Gonzalez, "Natural products as modulators of the proteostasis machinery: implications in neurodegenerative diseases," *International Journal of Molecular Sciences* 20, no. 19 (September 20, 2019): 4666, https://doi .org/10.3390/ijms20194666.

50. Y. R. Li, S. Li, and C. C. Lin, "Effect of resveratrol and pterostilbene on aging and longevity," *BioFactors* 44, no. 1 (January 2018): 69–82, https://doi.org/10.1002/biof.1400.

51. I. S. Pyo et al., "Mechanisms of aging and the preventive effects of resveratrol on age-related diseases," *Molecules* 25, no. 20 (October 12, 2020): 4649, https://doi.org/10.3390/molecules25204649.

52. D. D. Zhou et al., "Effects and mechanisms of resveratrol on aging and age-related diseases," *Oxidative Medicine and Cellular Longevity* 2021 (July 11, 2021): 9932218, https://doi.org/10.1155/2021/9932218.

53. "Selenium," The Nutrient Source, Harvard T. H. Chan School of Public Health, Harvard University, accessed 15 June 2022, https://www.hsph.harvard.edu/nutritionsource/selenium/#:~:text=Selenium%20is%20an%20essential%20component,the%20metabolism%20of%20thyroid%20hormones.

54. L. R. Ferguson et al., "Selenium and its role in the maintenance of genomic stability," *Mutation Research* 733, nos. 1–2 (May 1, 2012): 100–10, https://pubmed.ncbi.nlm.nih.gov/22234051.

55. Q. Wu et al., "Serine and metabolism regulation: a novel mechanism in antitumor immunity and senescence," *Aging and Disease* 11, no. 6 (December 1, 2020): 1640–53, https://doi.org/10.14336/AD.2020.0314.

56. R. A. Dunlop et al., "Mechanisms of L-serine neuroprotection in vitro include ER proteostasis regulation," *Neurotoxicity Research* 33, no. 1 (January 2018): 123–32, https://doi.org/10.1007/s12640-017-9829-3.

57. Q. Wu et al., "Serine and metabolism regulation: a novel mechanism in antitumor immunity and senescence," *Aging and Disease* 11, no. 6 (December 1, 2020): 1640–53, https://doi.org/10.14336/AD.2020.0314.

58. F. Madeo et al., "Spermidine delays aging in humans," *Aging* (Albany, NY) 10, no. 8 (2018): 2209–11, https://doi.org/10.18632/aging.101517.

59. F. Madeo et al., "Spermidine: a physiological autophagy inducer acting as an anti-aging vitamin in humans?" *Autophagy* 15, no. 1 (2019): 165–68, https://doi.org/10.1080/15548627.2018.1530929.

60. R. Santín-Márquez et al., "Sulforaphane—role in aging and neurodegeneration," *GeroScience* 41, no. 5 (2019): 655–70, https://doi.org/10.1007/s11357-019-00061-7.

61. S.-F. Kan, J. Wang, and G. X. Sun, "Sulforaphane regulates apoptosis- and proliferation-related signaling pathways and synergizes with cisplatin to suppress human ovarian cancer," *International Journal of Molecular Medicine* 42, no. 5 (2018): 2447–58, https://doi.org/10.3892/ijmm.2018.3860.

62. F. J. Schweigert et al., "Cats absorb β-carotene, but it is not converted to vitamin A," *The Journal of Nutrition* 132, no. 6 (2002): 1610S–1612S, https://doi.org/10.1093/jn/132.6.1610s.

63. K. Mikkelsen and V. Apostolopoulos, "B vitamins and ageing," *Subcellular Biochemistry* 90 (2018): 451–70, https://doi.org/10.1007/978-981-13-2835-0_15.

64. F. Monacelli et al., "Vitamin C, aging and Alzheimer's disease," *Nutrients* 9 no. 7 (June 27, 2017): 670, https://doi.org/10.3390/nu9070670.

65. S. Mumtaz et al., "Aging and its treatment with vitamin C: a comprehensive mechanistic review," *Molecular Biology Reports* 48, no. 12 (December 2021): 8141–53, https://doi.org/10.1007/s11033-021-06781-4.

66. B. Abiri and M. Vafa, "Vitamin D and muscle sarcopenia in aging," *Methods in Molecular Biology* 2138 (2020): 29–47, https://doi.org/10.1007/978-1-0716-0471-7_2.

67. C. Aranow, "Vitamin D and the immune system," *Journal of Investigative Medicine* 59, no. 6 (2011): 881–86, https://doi .org/10.2310/JIM.0b013e31821b8755.

68. H. Godman, "Vitamin D supplements may reduce risk of invasive cancer," Harvard Health, Harvard Medical School, June 1, 2021, https://www.health.harvard.edu/cancer/vitamin-d-supplements-may-reduce-risk-of-invasive-cancer.

69. M. Zarei et al., "The relationship between vitamin D and telomere/telomerase: a comprehensive review," *The Journal of Frailty & Aging* 10, no. 1 (2021): 2–9, https://doi.org/10.14283/jfa.2020.33.

70. S. Sirajudeen, I. Shah, and A. Al Menhali, "A narrative role of vitamin D and its receptor: with current evidence on the gastric tissues," *International Journal of Molecular Sciences* 20, no. 15 (August 5, 2019): 3832, https://doi.org/10.3390/ijms20153832.

71. Q. Zhang et al., "Evaluation of common genetic variants in vitamin E-related pathway genes and colorectal cancer susceptibility," *Archives of Toxicology* 95, no. 7 (July 2021): 2523–32, https://doi .org/10.1007/s00204-021-03078-0.

72. U. Mabalirajan et al., "Effects of vitamin E on mitochondrial dysfunction and asthma features in an experimental allergic murine model," *Journal of Applied Physiology* 107 no. 4 (2009): 1285–92, https://doi.org/10.1152/japplphysiol.00459.2009.

73. G. La Fata, P. Weber, and M. H. Mohajeri, "Effects of vitamin E on cognitive performance during ageing and in Alzheimer's disease," *Nutrients* 6, no. 12 (November 28, 2014): 5453–72, https://doi.org/10.3390/nu6125453.

74. M. Rhouma et al., "Anti-inflammatory response of dietary vitamin E and its effects on pain and joint structures during early stages of surgically induced osteoarthritis in dogs," *Canadian Journal of Veterinary Research* 77, no. 3 (2013): 191–98.

75. G. K., Schwalfenberg, "Vitamins K1 and K2: the emerging group of vitamins required for human health," *Journal of Nutrition and Metabolism* 2017 (June 18, 2017): 6254836, https://doi.org/10.1155/2017/6254836.

76. D. S. Popa, G. Bigman, and M. E. Rusu, "The role of vitamin K in humans: implication in aging and age-associated diseases," *Antioxidants* (Basel) 10, no. 4 (April 6, 2021): 566, https://doi.org/10.3390/antiox10040566.

77. D. S. Popa, G. Bigman, and M. E. Rusu, "The role of vitamin K in humans: implication in aging and age-associated diseases," *Antioxidants* (Basel) 10, no. 4 (April 6, 2021): 566, https://doi.org/10.3390/antiox10040566.

78. Á. J. R. Cabrera, "Zinc, aging, and immunosenescence: an overview," *Pathobiology of Aging & Age-Related Diseases* 5, no. 1 (February 5, 2015): 25592, https://doi.org/10.3402/pba.v5.25592.

79. X. Yang et al., "Zinc enhances the cellular energy supply to improve cell motility and restore impaired energetic metabolism in a toxic environment induced by OTA," *Scientific Reports* 7, no, 1 (November 7, 2017): 14669, https://doi.org/10.1038/s41598-017-14868-x.

Chapter 7

1. C. K. Sen, "Wound healing essentials: let there be oxygen," *Wound Repair and Regeneration* 17, no. 1 (January–February 2009): 1–18, https://doi.org/10.1111/j.1524-475X.2008.00436.x.

2. A. Valli, A. L. Harris, and B. M. Kessler, "Hypoxia metabolism in ageing," *Aging* (Albany, NY) 7, no. 7 (July 2015): 465– 66, https://doi.org/10.18632/aging.100782.

3. S. M. Welford and A. J. Giaccia, "Hypoxia and senescence: the impact of oxygenation on tumor suppression," *Molecular Cancer Research* 9, no. 5 (May 2011): 538–44, https://doi.org/10.1158/1541-7786.MCR-11-0065.

4. A. Simpson, "Compressed air as a therapeutic agent in the treatment of consumption, asthma, chronic bronchitis and other diseases," *Glasgow Medical Journal* 5, no. 17 (1857): 94–96.

5. S. Tejada et al., "Therapeutic effects of hyperbaric oxygen in the process of wound healing," *Current Pharmaceutical Design* 25, no. 15 (2019): 1682–93, https://doi.org/10.2174/1381612825666190703162648.

6. B. B. Hart, "Hyperbaric oxygen for refractory osteomyelitis," *Undersea & Hyperbaric Medicine* 48, no. 3 (third quarter 2021): 297–321.

7. Q. Z. Lu et al., "Further application of hyperbaric oxygen in prostate cancer," *Medical Gas Research* 8, no. 4 (January 9, 2019): 167–71, https://doi.org/10.4103/2045-9912.248268.

8. I. Moen and L. E. B. Stuhr, "Hyperbaric oxygen therapy and cancer—a review," *Targeted Oncology* 7, no. 4 (December 2012): 233–42, https://doi.org/10.1007/s11523-012-0233-x.

9. S.-Y. Chen et al., "Hyperbaric oxygen suppressed tumor progression through the improvement of tumor hypoxia and induction of tumor apoptosis in A549-cell-transferred lung cancer," *Scientific Reports* 11, no. 1 (June 8, 2021): 12033, https://doi.org/10.1038/s41598-021-91454-2.

10. Y. Hachmo et al., "Hyperbaric oxygen therapy increases telomere length and decreases immunosenescence in isolated blood cells: a prospective trial," *Aging* (Albany, NY) 12, no. 22 (November 18, 2020): 22445–56, https://doi.org/10.18632/aging.202188.

11. I. Peña-Villalobos et al., "Hyperbaric oxygen increases stem cell proliferation, angiogenesis and wound-healing ability of WJ-MSCs in diabetic mice," *Frontiers in Physiology* 9 (July 30, 2018): 995, https://doi.org/10.3389/fphys.2018.00995.

12. A. Hadanny et al., "Hyperbaric oxygen therapy induces transcriptome changes in elderly: a prospective trial," *Aging* (Albany, NY) 13, no. 22 (November 24, 2021): 24511–23, https://doi .org/10.18632/aging.203709.

13. A. Hadanny et al., "Cognitive enhancement of healthy older adults using hyperbaric oxygen: a randomized controlled trial," *Aging* (Albany, NY) 12, no. 13 (June 26, 2020): 13740–61, https://doi .org/10.18632/aging.103571.

14. F. J. Hidalgo-Tallón et al., "Updated review on ozone therapy in pain medicine," *Frontiers in Physiology* 13 (February 23, 2022): 840623, https://doi.org/10.3389/fphys.2022.840623.

15. N. L. Smith et al., "Ozone therapy: an overview of pharmacodynamics, current research, and clinical utility," *Medical Gas Research* 7, no. 3 (October 17, 2017): 212–19, https://doi .org/10.4103/2045-9912.215752.

16. C. Scassellati et al., "Ozone: a natural bioactive molecule with antioxidant property as potential new strategy in aging and in neurodegenerative disorders," *Ageing Research Reviews* 63 (November 2020): 101138, https://doi.org/10.1016/j.arr.2020.101138.

17. S. Tang et al., "Ozone induces BEL7402 cell apoptosis by increasing reactive oxygen species production and activating JNK," *Annals of Translational Medicine* 9, no, 15 (August 2021): 1257, https://doi .org/10.21037/atm-21-3233.

18. B. Clavo et al., "Ozone therapy as adjuvant for cancer treatment: is further research warranted?," *Evidence-Based Complementary and Alternative Medicine* 2018 (September 9, 2018): 7931849, https://doi .org/10.1155/2018/7931849.

19. Hidalgo-Tallón et al., "Updated review on ozone therapy in pain medicine."

20. Smith et al., "Ozone therapy."

21. Scassellati et al., "Ozone: a natural bioactive molecule."

22. Tang, "Ozone induces BEL7402 cell apoptosis."
23. Clavo, "Ozone therapy as adjuvant for cancer treatment."
24. K. Sharun et al., "Therapeutic potential of platelet-rich plasma in canine medicine," *Archives of Razi Institute* 76, no. 4 (September–October 2021): 721–30, https://doi.org/10.22092/ari.2021.355953.1749.
25. Encyclopaedia Britannica Online, s.v. "capillary," updated July 23, 2019, https://www.britannica.com/science/capillary.
26. E. Eggenhofer et al., "Mesenchymal stem cells are short-lived and do not migrate beyond the lungs after intravenous infusion," *Frontiers in Immunology* 3 (September 26, 2012): 297, https://doi.org/10.3389/fimmu.2012.00297.
27. E. Bari et al., "Mesenchymal stem/stromal cell secretome for lung regeneration: the long way through 'pharmaceuticalization' for the best formulation," *Journal of Controlled Release* 309 (September 10, 2019): 11–24, https://doi.org/10.1016/j.jconrel.2019.07.022.
28. D. M. L. W. Kruk, "Mesenchymal stromal cells to regenerate emphysema: on the horizon?," *Respiration* 96, no. 2 (2018): 148–58, https://doi.org/10.1159/000488149.
29. M. Z. Ratajczak et al., "Very small embryonic-like (VSEL) stem cells: purification from adult organs, characterization, and biological significance," *Stem Cell Reviews* 4, no. 2 (summer 2008): 89–99, https://doi.org/10.1007/s12015-008-9018-0.
30. M. Z. Ratajczak, J. Ratajczak, and M. Kucia, "Very small embryonic-like stem cells (VSELs): an update and future directions," *Circulation Research* 124, no. 2 (January 17, 2019), https://www.ahajournals .org/doi/10.1161/CIRCRESAHA.118.314287#:~:text=Evidence%20has%20accumulated%20that%20VSELs,cells%2C%20and%20endothelial%20progenitor%20cells.
31. Ratajczak, Ratajczak, and Kucia, "Very small embryonic-like stem cells (VSELs)."
32. P. Hollands, D. R. Aboyeji, and T. Ovokaitys, "The action of modulated laser light on Human Very Small Embryonic Like (hVSEL) stem cells in Platelet Rich Plasma (PRP)," *CellR4* 8 (2020): e2990, https://doi.org/10.32113/cellr4_202012_2990.
33. J. Brindley, P. Hollands, and T. Ovokaitys, "A theoretical mechanism for the action of SONG-modulated laser light on Human Very Small Embryonic-Like (hVSEL) stem cells in Platelet Rich Plasma (PRP)," *CellR4* 9 (2021): e3201, https://doi.org/10.32113/cellr4_20216_3201.
34. E. K. Zuba-Surma et al., "Very small embryonic-like stem cells: biology and therapeutic potential for heart repair," *Antioxidant & Redox Signaling* 15, no. 7 (October 1, 2011): 1821–34, https://doi .org/10.1089/ars.2010.3817.

35. M. Z. Ratajczak et al., "Very small embryonic-like (VSEL) stem cells in adult organs and their potential role in rejuvenation of tissues and longevity," *Experimental Gerontology* 43, no. 11 (November 2008): 1009–17, https://doi.org/10.1016/j.exger.2008.06.002.

36. P. Han et al., "The association between intestinal bacteria and allergic diseases—cause or consequence?," *Frontiers in Cellular and Infection Microbiology* 11 (April 15, 2021): 650893, https://doi .org/10.3389/fcimb.2021.650893.

37. K. L. Tooley, "Effects of the human gut microbiota on cognitive performance, brain structure and function: a narrative review," *Nutrients* 12, no. 10 (September 30, 2020): 3009, https://doi.org/10.3390/nu12103009.

38. J. Liu et al., "Gut microbiota approach—a new strategy to treat Parkinson's disease," *Frontiers in Cellular and Infection Microbiology* 10 (October 22, 2020): 570658, https://doi.org/10.3389/fcimb.2020.570658.

39. O. C. Aroniadis and L. J. Brandt, "Intestinal microbiota and the efficacy of fecal microbiota transplantation in gastrointestinal disease," *Gastroenterology & Hepatology* 10, no. 4 (April 2014): 230–37.

40. "Fecal transplants restore gut microbes after antibiotics," NIH Research Matters, National Institutes of Health, Bethesda, MD, October 16, 2018, https://www.nih.gov/news-events/nih-research-matters/fecal-transplants-restore-gut-microbes-after-antibiotics.

41. A. Parker et al., "Fecal microbiota transfer between young and aged mice reverses hallmarks of the aging gut, eye, and brain," *Microbiome* 10, no. 1 (April 29, 2022): 68, https://doi.org/10.1186/s40168-022-01243-w.

42. M. J. Conboy, I. M. Conboy, and T. A. Rando, "Heterochronic parabiosis: historical perspective and methodological considerations for studies of aging and longevity," *Aging Cell* 12, no. 3 (June 2013): 525–30, https://doi.org/10.1111/acel.12065.

43. M. Mehdipour et al., "Rejuvenation of three germ layers tissues by exchanging old blood plasma with saline-albumin," *Aging* (Albany, NY) 12, no. 10 (May 30, 2020): 8790–819, https://doi.org/10.18632/aging.103418.

44. M. Mehdipour et al., "Plasma dilution improves cognition and attenuates neuroinflammation in old mice," *GeroScience* 43, no. 1 (February 2021): 1–18, https://doi.org/10.1007/s11357-020-00297-8.

45. M. V. Blagosklonny, "Rapamycin for longevity: opinion article," *Aging* (Albany, NY) 11, no. 19 (October 4, 2019): 8048–67, https://doi.org/10.18632/aging.102355.

46. R. Selvarani, S. Mohammed, and A. Richardson, "Effect of rapamycin on aging and age-related diseases—past and future," *GeroScience* 43, no. 3 (June 2021): 1135–58, https://doi.org/10.1007/s11357-020-00274-1.

47. "Dog Aging Project goal is to help both dogs and humans live longer, healthier lives," National Institute on Aging, National Institutes of Health, Bethesda, MD, February 24, 2022, https://www.nia.nih.gov/news/dog-aging-project-goal-help-both-dogs-and-humans-live-longer-healthier-lives.

48. C. López-Otín et al., "The hallmarks of aging," *Cell* 153, no. 6 (June 6, 2013): 1194–217, https://doi.org/10.1016/j.cell.2013.05.039.

49. S. Zeng, W. H. Shen, and L. Liu, "Senescence and cancer," *Cancer Translational Medicine* 4, no. 3 (May–June 2018): 70–74, https://pubmed.ncbi.nlm.nih.gov/30766922.

50. M. Xu et al., "Senolytics improve physical function and increase lifespan in old age." *Nature Medicine* 24, no. 8 (August 2018): 1246–56, https://doi.org/10.1038/s41591-018-0092-9.

51. M. B. Cavalcante et al., "Dasatinib plus quercetin prevents uterine age-related dysfunction and fibrosis in mice," *Aging* (Albany, NY) 12, no. 3 (January 18, 2020): 2711–22, https://doi.org/10.18632/aging.102772.

52. E. J. Novais et al., "Long-term treatment with senolytic drugs Dasatinib and Quercetin ameliorates age-dependent intervertebral disc degeneration in mice," *Nature Communications* 12, no. 1 (September 3, 2021): 5213, https://doi.org/10.1038/s41467-021-25453-2.

53. J. L. Kirkland and T. Tchkonia, "Senolytic drugs: from discovery to translation," *Journal of Internal Medicine* 288, no. 5 (November 2020): 518–36, https://doi.org/10.1111/joim.13141.

54. S. Seiwerth et al., "Stable gastric pentadecapeptide BPC 157 and wound healing," *Frontiers in Pharmacology* 12 (June 29, 2021): 627533, https://doi.org/10.3389/fphar.2021.627533.

55. D. Gwyer, N. M. Wragg, and S. L. Wilson, "Gastric pentadecapeptide body protection compound BPC 157 and its role in accelerating musculoskeletal soft tissue healing," *Cell and Tissue Research* 377, no. 2 (August 2019): 153–59, https://doi.org/10.1007/s00441-019-03016-8.

56. P. Sikiric, "Brain-gut axis and pentadecapeptide BPC 157: theoretical and practical implications," *Current Neuropharmacology* 14, no. 8 (2016): 857–65, https://doi.org/10.2174/1570159x13666160502153022.

57. A. L. Goldstein et al., "Thymosin β4: a multi-functional regenerative peptide. Basic properties and clinical applications," *Expert Opinion on Biological Therapy* 12, no. 1 (January 2012): 37–51, https://doi.org/10.1517/14712598.2012.634793.

58. G. T. Pipes and J. Yang, "Cardioprotection by thymosin beta 4," *Vitamins and Hormones* 102 (2016): 209–26, https://doi.org/10.1016/bs.vh.2016.04.004.

59. G. Sosne, "Thymosin beta 4 and the eye: the journey from bench to bedside," *Expert Opinion on Biological Therapy* 18, suppl. 1 (2018): 99–104, https://doi.org/10.1080/14712598.2018.1486818.

60. J. Kim and Y. Jung, "Thymosin beta 4 is a potential regulator of hepatic stellate cells," *Vitamins and Hormones* 102 (2016): 121–49, https://doi.org/10.1016/bs.vh.2016.04.011.

61. K. Maar et al., "Utilizing developmentally essential secreted peptides such as thymosin beta-4 to remind the adult organs of their embryonic state—new directions in anti-aging regenerative therapies," *Cells* 10, no. 6 (May 28, 2021): 1343, https://doi.org/10.3390/cells10061343.

62. Y. Zhang et al., "Thymosin Beta 4 is overexpressed in human pancreatic cancer cells and stimulates proinflammatory cytokine secretion and JNK activation," *Cancer Biology & Therapy* 7, no. 3 (March 2008): 419–23, https://doi.org/10.4161/cbt.7.3.5415.

63. J. Caers et al., "Thymosin β4 has tumor suppressive effects and its decreased expression results in poor prognosis and decreased survival in multiple myeloma," *Haematologica* 95, no. 1 (January 2010): 163–67, https://doi.org/10.3324/haematol.2009.006411.

64. G. Sosne and H. K. Kleinman, "Primary mechanisms of thymosin β4 repair activity in dry eye disorders and other tissue injuries," *Investigative Ophthalmology & Visual Science* 56, no. 9 (August 2015): 5110–17, https://doi.org/10.1167/iovs.15-16890.

65. S. L. Teichman et al., "Prolonged stimulation of growth hormone (GH) and insulin-like growth factor I secretion by CJC-1295, a long-acting analog of GH-releasing hormone, in healthy adults," *The Journal of Clinical Endocrinology & Metabolism* 91, no. 3 (March 2006): 799–805, https://doi.org/10.1210/jc.2005-1536.

66. M. Alba et al., "Once-daily administration of CJC-1295, a long-acting growth hormone-releasing hormone (GHRH) analog, normalizes growth in the GHRH knockout mouse," *AJP Endocrinology and Metabolism* 291, no. 6 (December 2006): E1290-4, https://doi.org/10.1152/ajpendo.00201.2006.

67. K. Raun et al., "Ipamorelin, the first selective growth hormone secretagogue," *European Journal of Endocrinology* 139, no. 5 (November 1998): 552–61, https://pubmed.ncbi.nlm.nih .gov/9849822.

INDEX

NOTE: Page references in italics refer to figures.

D

E

S

Y

Z

ACKNOWLEDGMENTS

Support in writing this book came from multiple sources, including some of the world's leading longevity physicians: Dr. Jeffery Gladden, Dr. Todd Ovokaitys, Dr. Matthew Cook, and Dr. Harry McIlroy. Thanks also to Richard Rossi, whose ability to gather the brightest minds in longevity science in one room has provided me with knowledge that benefits me, my family, my patients, and now you. Thanks also to Jessica Bogosian, the best veterinary technician and manager there is, and the team at Holistic Veterinary Care, who provide better care for pets than most people ever receive.

This book would not have happened without the love and support of my wife, Lee, who is unquestionably the best networker and connector of people on the planet. Without her, I would never have had the opportunity to meet the brilliant minds in science and medicine who have made me a better veterinarian. Special thanks also go to my ever-supportive and wonderful daughter, Abbey, who makes my life better every day.

ABOUT THE AUTHOR

Gary Richter, M.S., D.V.M., C.V.C., C.V.A., has been practicing veterinary medicine in the San Francisco Bay Area since 1998. In addition to conventional veterinary medical training, Dr. Richter is certified in veterinary acupuncture and veterinary chiropractic. As owner and medical director of Holistic Veterinary Care in Oakland, California, he understands the benefits of both conventional and holistic treatment methods for the preventive and the therapeutic care of pets.

Dr. Richter focuses on the integration of holistic and general-practice veterinary medicine and regenerative medicine, as well as educating professionals and pet owners on the benefits of integrative care. By combining medical cannabis with other conventional and alternative therapies, he has been able to improve the quality and quantity of life of pets living with medical conditions ranging from arthritis to inflammatory bowel disease to cancer.

The past president of the American College of Veterinary Botanical Medicine and a founding member of the Veterinary Cannabis Society, Dr. Richter has written numerous articles for print and web publications on various topics, including strategies to integrate the use of medical cannabis into conventional medical therapies for pets. His first book, *The Ultimate Pet Health Guide*, was released in 2017.

Dr. Richter's current focus is on providing information on pet health and longevity to pet owners worldwide using virtual platforms; offering highly effective, natural supplements and food for pets through his company Ultimate Pet Nutrition; and creating a wearable biometric monitor for animals through his company PetMetrics. Visit him at www.longevityforpets.com or www.ultimatepetnutrition.com.

Hay House Titles of Related Interest

YOU CAN HEAL YOUR LIFE, the movie,
starring Louise Hay & Friends
(available as an online streaming video)
www.hayhouse.com/louise-movie

THE SHIFT, the movie,
starring Dr. Wayne W. Dyer
(available as an online streaming video)
www.hayhouse.com/the-shift-movie

***

ANIMAL COMMUNICATION MADE EASY: Strengthen Your Bond and Deepen Your Connection with Animals, by Pea Horsley

ANIMAL MAGIC: The Extraordinary Proof of our Pets' Intuition and Unconditional Love for Us, by Gordon Smith

BEYOND LONGEVITY: A Proven Plan for Healing Faster, Feeling Better, and Thriving at Any Age, by Jason Prall

DOGS AND CATS HAVE SOULS TOO: Incredible True Stories of Pets Who Heal, Protect, and Communicate, by Jenny Smedley

NATURAL NUTRITION FOR CATS: The Path to Purr-fect Health, by Kymythy Schultze, C.C.N., A.H.I.

All of the above are available at your local bookstore, or may be ordered by contacting Hay House (see next page).

***

We hope you enjoyed this Hay House book. If you'd like to receive our online catalog featuring additional information on Hay House books and products, or if you'd like to find out more about the Hay Foundation, please contact:

Hay House, Inc., P.O. Box 5100, Carlsbad, CA 92018-5100
(760) 431-7695 or (800) 654-5126
(760) 431-6948 (fax) or (800) 650-5115 (fax)
www.hayhouse.com® • www.hayfoundation.org

Published in Australia by: Hay House Australia Pty. Ltd.,
18/36 Ralph St., Alexandria NSW 2015
Phone: 612-9669-4299 • *Fax:* 612-9669-4144
www.hayhouse.com.au

Published in the United Kingdom by: Hay House UK, Ltd.,
The Sixth Floor, Watson House, 54 Baker Street, London W1U 7BU
Phone: +44 (0)20 3927 7290 • *Fax:* +44 (0)20 3927 7291
www.hayhouse.co.uk

Published in India by: Hay House Publishers India,
Muskaan Complex, Plot No. 3, B-2, Vasant Kunj, New Delhi 110 070
Phone: 91-11-4176-1620
www.hayhouse.co.in
